PRACTICAL APPROACHES TO INDIVIDUALIZING STAFF DEVELOPMENT FOR ADULTS

~

Edited by
Rita Dunn and Kenneth Dunn

PRAEGER

Westport, Connecticut
London

Library of Congress Cataloging-in-Publication Data

Practical approaches to indivdualizing staff development for adults
/ edited by Rita Dunn and Kenneth Dunn.
    p.   cm.
    Includes bibliographical references and index.
    ISBN 0–275–96066–8 (alk. paper)
    1. Employees—Training of. I. Dunn, Kenneth J. II. Dunn, Rita
Stafford, 1930.
    HF5549.5.T7P6288 1998
    658.3′124—DC21   97–33710

British Library Cataloguing in Publication Data is available.

Library of Congress Catalog Card Number: 97–33710
ISBN: 0–275–96066–8

First published in 1998

Praeger Publishers, 88 Post Road West, Westport, CT 06881
An imprint of Greenwood Publishing Group, Inc.

Printed in the United States of America

The paper used in this book complies with the
Permanent Paper Standard issued by the National
Information Standards Organization (Z39.48–1984).

10 9 8 7 6 5 4 3 2 1

Contents

Introduction: What's Wrong with the Experts' Guidelines?

Articles and books often propose that the people for whom staff development is intended do not appreciate it because they

- *have not been actively involved in the planning.* However, a survey of your own agency, building, department, district, or institution is likely to reveal that some people want to be involved, but many do not.

- *have little interest in the topic.* Odds are strong that some people are interested in almost any new topic whereas others are rarely interested in any.

- *previously experienced a motivating speaker, became interested, if not enthusiastic, and then were given no follow-up assistance in translating the idea or theory into practice.* That tends to be accurate. However, some adults want help when implementing ideas and others do not.

- *are asked to try several new approaches during the same period.* That also may be accurate. However, some people like being exposed to many new things simultaneously, whereas others cannot tolerate multiple exposures regardless of whether or not they choose to try any.

- *find that new approaches come and go.* They reason that it makes little sense to exert themselves for a fad that is likely to be "old hat" next year!

- *believe nobody really cares if there is follow-up.* Perhaps their administrators, staff developers, and supervisors do care, but chances are good that they do not show it in all the ways that diverse individuals understand. To some, caring means that you work side by side with them to adopt a new strategy— and stay with it until either it works or you both agree that it won't. To others, caring means being left alone to do what they choose because you trust their ability.

Thus, unless you are fully aware of the differences among how individuals perceive staff development, there will always be some who applaud—and some who resist or scorn—whatever is planned. This book is devoted to making staff development interesting to, and effective with, many different practitioners. It describes practical and inexpensive ways of individualizing staff development by capitalizing on adults' individual learning styles.

PART I

ADULT LEARNING STYLES:
A FOUNDATION FOR
STAFF DEVELOPMENT

Teaching Adults through Their Learning-Style Strengths: A Choice Approach

Rita Dunn

Today is another superintendent's conference day—the umpteenth in your career. A keynote speech is scheduled for the morning and you have a choice of workshops in the afternoon. Regardless of the speaker or consultant, chances are good that all sessions will be taught traditionally—everyone attending will learn the same thing in the same way at the same time and in the same amount of time. What's more, each session will be pretty much like every other session—with only the speaker's delivery and topic changing.

It's no wonder that many adults feel little other than resignation about staff development. In any group, more than half the people attending learn differently from the way the speaker presents. Once that mismatch occurs, the presentation quickly becomes ho-hum—if not downright boring—unless the presenter is dynamic and humorous. Even then, entertainment without learning is the result. What can people who are responsible for staff development do to increase the attractiveness of sessions and to ensure that participants learn from attending? The first step would be to become acquainted with learning style.

INTRODUCTION TO LEARNING STYLE

Human beings have many similar traits, but how they learn new or difficult information is as unique as their individual fingerprints. How people learn is called their *learning style*. Many people can learn things that are easy for them without using their learning styles, but all people learn new and difficult information better when they capitalize on their styles. Because at every age, people learn more, do so more easily, and retain it better when they use their learning styles, their styles are actually their strengths (Dunn, Griggs, Olson, Beasley, & Gorman, 1995).

Differences in how individuals learn explain why, in the same family, some do well in school while others do not. Those differences also explain why no single instructional method or resource "works" well for everyone. Although each approach helps some learners achieve, that same strategy inhibits learning for others.

Conventional Staff Development

Conventional staff development often requires that participants sit quietly in their seats for an hour or more and learn by either listening to the speaker, reading materials, or both. Occasionally, participants are divided into small groups to learn through interactions with others or to see a filmstrip, movie, or video. Sometimes, participants are asked to develop a project. Regardless of how the staff development has been planned, where it takes place and how the participants are taught are usually the same for all. Everyone is expected to learn in exactly the same way that everyone else learns.

Learning-Style-Based Staff Development

When staff development is based on a learning-style approach, the same information is introduced in alternative ways and participants choose to learn through the resources or approaches most closely matched to their style. For example, in one study, secondary school teachers used the new instructional strategies they were taught at their most preferred time of day more frequently than the strategies they were taught at their less preferred time of day (Dunn, Dunn, & Freeley, 1984).

What Exactly Is Learning Style?

Learning style is the way each person begins to concentrate on, process, and retain new and difficult information. Concentration occurs differently for different people at different times of the day. It is important to identify individuals' styles to trigger their concentration, energize their processing, and increase their long-term memory.

HOW DO WE IDENTIFY ADULTS' LEARNING STYLES?

It is difficult to identify learning style accurately without a reliable instrument (Beaty, 1986; Dunn, Dunn, & Price, 1977; Marcus, 1977); some traits are not observable and others lend themselves to misinterpretation. For example, if two persons sitting next to each other during a presentation chew gum, whisper, squirm in their seats, and pay little attention to the speaker, an observer could not determine whether they are uninterested, anti-authoritarian, nonconforming, kinesthetic, unable to sit in the available chairs, hungry, or in need of an informal design or mobility.

Thus, to identify how individuals learn, it is necessary to use a comprehensive instrument—one that diagnoses many different learning-style traits. Only three comprehensive models exist, and each has a related instrument designed to reveal individuals' styles based on the variables included in that model (DeBello, 1990).

In addition to being comprehensive, an instrument must also be reliable and valid. That is, a reliable instrument provides consistent information over time; a valid instrument measures what its research manual says it does. Instrument reliability and validity are crucial because it is impossible to obtain accurate data from an unreliable or invalid assessment.

Instrument 1: The Productivity Environmental Preference Survey

The most frequently used learning-style instrument in experimental studies with adults is the Dunn, Dunn, and Price (1982) Productivity Environmental Preference Survey (PEPS). PEPS and the Learning Style Inventory, its counterpart for children, have been used in research conducted at more than 100 institutions of higher education (Research on the Dunn & Dunn Model, 1997).

PEPS reports how strongly 20 different learning-style elements affect each person (see Table 1.1).

Instrument 2: Business Excellence

A new, recently field-tested instrument, Business Excellence (BE), was specifically designed to identify the learning styles of adults in corporate and industrial firms (Rundle & Dunn, 1996). Developed cooperatively by St. John's University's Center for the Study of Learning and Teaching Styles and Performance Contracts, a business firm, BE can be administered and hand-scored on site within a 20 to 30-minute period and has the advantage of permitting presenters to identify either one, several, or all of its 21 learning-style elements—including global versus analytic cognitive processing styles. In addition, BE includes a short global introduction to each element and also provides short descriptions of how to increase productivity based on the analyses of each person's style.

As Figure 1.1 illustrates, BE reports on each individual's

- *environmental* preferences for sound or quiet, low versus bright light, warm versus cool temperatures, and informal versus formal seating designs while concentrating on demanding tasks
- *emotional* preferences concerned with high or low motivation, persistence as opposed to needing breaks while concentrating, conformity versus nonconformity, and internal versus external need for structure
- *sociological* preferences for learning alone, in a pair, with peers, in a small group, with an authoritative versus a collegial presenter, or in varied ways as opposed to in a pattern or routine
- *physiological* preferences, such as the perceptual modalities through which he or she best remembers new and difficult academic information, for example, by hearing versus seeing versus manipulating materials with one's hands versus

Table 1.1
Productivity Environmental Preference Survey Elements

Environmental Elements

   1. Noise level   Silence versus sound

   2. Light   Dim versus bright light

   3. Temperature   Cool versus warm temperature

   4. Design   Informal versus formal seating

Emotional Elements

   5. Motivation   Self-motivated

   6. Persistence   Persistence versus periodic breaks

   7. Responsibility   Conformity versus nonconformity

   8. Structure   Internal versus external structure

Sociological Elements

   9. Alone/peer   Learning alone versus peer-oriented learner

 10. Authority figures   Authority figures absent/present
                                   Requiring versus not requiring feedback

 11. Several ways   Requiring patterns and routines versus variety

Physiological Elements

 12. Auditory   Remembers $\frac{3}{4}$ of what is heard

 13. Visual   Remembers $\frac{3}{4}$ of what is read/seen

 14. Tactile   Remembers $\frac{3}{4}$ of what is written/manipulated

 15. Kinesthetic   Remembers $\frac{3}{4}$ of what is experienced

 16. Intake   Learns best while eating/drinking

 17. Evening—morning   Evening versus morning alert

 18. Late morning   Functions best in late morning

 19. Afternoon   Functions best in afternoon

 20. Mobility   Learning while passive versus mobile

Figure 1.1
Learning Styles Model

Stimuli   Elements

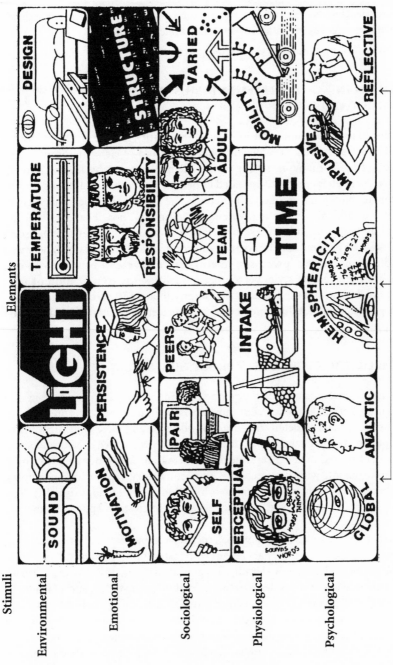

Environmental   SOUND   LIGHT   TEMPERATURE   DESIGN

Emotional   MOTIVATION   PERSISTENCE   RESPONSIBILITY   STRUCTURE

Sociological   SELF   PAIR   PEERS   TEAM   ADULT   VARIED

Physiological   PERCEPTUAL   INTAKE   TIME   MOBILITY

Psychological   GLOBAL   ANALYTIC   HEMISPHERICITY   IMPULSIVE   REFLECTIVE

Simultaneous or Successive Processing

Designed by Dr. Rita Dunn and Dr. Kenneth Dunn.

experiencing; the time of day each person concentrates best; and the individual's preferences for intake or mobility while concentrating

- *processing-style* preferences, as required by analytics and globals

WHICH LEARNING-STYLE ELEMENTS MUST BE ACCOMMODATED?

Of the 20 to 21 elements that PEPS and BE identify, no one is affected by all; most people are affected by somewhere between 5 and 14 elements. Some adults are affected by as many as 16 (or more) elements; many by fewer (2 to 6). However, every element that is revealed as being a preference or a strong preference for an individual is likely to increase the ease with which that person concentrates and his or her enjoyment of doing so. Those elements that are revealed as being an individual's preferences combine to form that person's "style." All style elements are important and contribute differentially to how well each adult concentrates, processes, internalizes, and retains new and difficult information. Processing style, perceptual modalities, the combination of light and seating design, and time of day affect approximately 70 percent of all people. Sound, persistence, mobility, and sociological preferences also affect large clusters of people.

THE IMPLICATIONS OF ADULTS' PROCESSING STYLES

The terms *analytic* and *global* describe how individuals begin to take in and process information. Analytics learn most easily when information is presented in step-by-step, sequenced details that gradually develop cognitive understanding of a concept. On the other hand, globals learn more easily when they either understand the concept first and then concentrate on the details, or when they are introduced to the information with, preferably, a humorous story replete with examples, applications, and graphics related to their lives. Most presentations usually follow a step-by-step, detailed lecture approach which, if interesting, appeals to analytic learners.

Whether people are analytic or global, they seem capable of mastering identical information or skills when they are taught with instructional methods or resources that complement their styles (Dunn, Griggs, Olson, Beasley, & Gorman, 1995). Thus, staff development needs to be provided both analytically and globally. In addition, global people seem to require a different learning environment from conventional classrooms or an auditorium, library, or gymnasium. Globals also require nurturing when they need a break from work and encouragement to stay on task, in addition to shorter, rather than longer, tasks because of their comparatively low persistence levels while concentrating on academics.

Although many adults retain complex information when what they are learning is interesting to them, globals neither concentrate academically nor stay on task unless the information is both interesting and related to their lives.

Therefore, caution consultants to begin their presentation with a short, humorous (if possible) anecdote that directly relates the focus of the session or the program to the participants' lives or experiences. Encourage the use of colored pictures and graphics to accompany short, attractive text or illustrations on transparencies, slides, discs, films, or PowerPoint™. Involve the participants in the presentation whenever possible—perhaps in periodic discussion, demonstrations, paired or small-group strategies, responses to queries, or written exercises.

THE IMPLICATIONS OF ADULTS' ENVIRONMENTAL PREFERENCES

Staff developers need to become aware of the environment in which they conduct staff development sessions and control it to the extent that they can. Given the knowledge that individuals require different kinds and degrees of quiet and sound, light, temperature, and seating, it is their responsibility to provide alternative areas where people can congregate to learn—for that is how staff development should begin.

Although analytic participants usually require quiet while concentrating on complex information, many globals tend to learn better with sound. For global adults, baroque music, smooth jazz, and quiet new age music usually work best to increase concentration than melodies with words. However, remember to maintain quiet in the section of the environment where analytics will be learning.

Take the time to experiment with the lighting so that the area has both brighter and more dimly illuminated sections. Scout out the room to be certain that it is neither too cool or too warm. If it is, seek assistance in moderating the temperature. If you try but find that you can't do anything about it, have the courtesy to alert people to bring extra clothing (if it is too cold) or to wear less (if it is too warm). Check for variations of temperature, such as drafts or air conditioning blowers within the room or the need for fans. Remember, some participants will feel cold, others comfortable, and still others warm in the same environment.

Examine the setup well before people arrive. Provide different types of furniture—an easy chair or two, a couple of couches, some bean bags for the adults who enjoy extremely casual designs, and some pillows for the chairs. You might even appropriate a couple of light blankets. People will appreciate your effort to make them comfortable.

THE IMPLICATIONS OF ADULTS' SOCIOLOGICAL PREFERENCES

Don't prejudge that people will either want to work in groups or learn directly from the presenter during the session. Provide choices and encourage people to make their own decisions concerning how to proceed. Neither cooperative learning nor direct instruction will please a majority of participants who attend any meeting. Sociological preferences are so varied that, in almost any group of 150 or more, approximately 28 percent may enjoy working either in pairs or in a small group;

another 28 percent will prefer either a collegial or an authoritative presenter; almost 13 percent prefer learning independently with appropriate resources but without people nearby; and the remainder either like variety or find that their preferences vary depending on the speaker and/or the topic.

Respect the participants' individuality, make everyone aware that learning-style differences exist, and provide options. Providing alternatives does not imply that everyone experience all the choices. Dignify people by allowing them to do it their way as long as they (1) do not distract anyone else from concentrating and (2) complete the objectives established for the session.

THE IMPLICATIONS OF PERCEPTUAL PREFERENCES

That individuals remember differently the complex information they learn by hearing, reading or seeing, tactually manipulating, or experiencing may be one of the major findings of this era. Previously, it was believed that most people could learn almost anything if they would only "sit still and pay attention!" We now know that this is a false assumption.

When adults were introduced to new material through their perceptual preferences, they remembered significantly more than when they were introduced to similar material through their least preferred modality (Ingham, 1991). They also enjoyed learning more from presenters with similar perceptual strengths (Buell & Buell, 1987).

Many adult males are not auditory. Only a small percentage of males of any age remember three-quarters of what they hear in a normal 40–50-minute period. As a result, lectures, discussions, and listening are the least effective strategy for teaching many males. However, even among females, less than 30 percent are auditory learners.

If people are not auditory learners, are they visual? Visual resources help many people learn, but many men and some women learn best with their hands (tactually) and through experience (kinesthetically). Once you identify tactual learners, you can reach them and hold their attention with the resources Roger Callan describes in Chapter 12. However, to respond to kinesthetic learners, read about Diane Mitchell's and Eileen D'Anna's floor games in Chapter 13. And if you have to provide training for nonconforming, anti-authoritarian, and uncollaborative staff, don't miss Marjorie Schiering's and Rita Taylor's Multisensory Instructional Packages (MIP) in Chapter 14. MIPs really work when all else fails!

THE IMPLICATIONS OF ADULTS' TIME-OF-DAY PREFERENCES

Task efficiency is greatest when each adult has the most energy to concentrate on difficult material. For example, in one study, teachers' time preferences were identified and staff development sessions were conducted in both matched and mismatched sessions. Those high school teachers used instructional strategies that they had been exposed to during staff development significantly more often when they attended sessions during their preferred time of day in contrast to when they attended sessions during their nonpreferred times (Dunn, Dunn, & Freeley, 1984; Freeley, 1984).

Whereas 55 percent of the adults we have tested appear to be early morning preferents, most staff development is conducted in the afternoon—adults' worst time of day. And we rarely address the 28 percent of adults who are "night owls."

Professional adults are involved in cognitive stretching almost all the time. For them to devote undiluted attention to staff development requires energy. Therefore, offer them choices of when they may attend staff development sessions and honor their decisions. Also, aim for staff development on nonworking days.

THE IMPLICATIONS OF ADULTS' RESTLESSNESS AND HYPERACTIVITY

Most adults who appear restless or inattentive during staff development are not clinically hyperactive. Instead, they often are in need of mobility, an informal design, a different approach to learning, or a presenter whose teaching style better matches their learning styles. In addition, the less interested adults are in what they are being taught, the more mobility they need. A disquieting point is that such persons are almost always males (Restak, 1979).

Add to this information the knowledge that between 40 and 50 percent of many adults require informal seating while concentrating and it is not difficult to understand why so many males squirm, extend their feet into aisles, squirrel down into their seats, and leave before the session is ended.

Staff developers need to establish several different instructional activity centers or areas in each environment so that mobility-preferenced adults who complete one task may move to another area to work on the next.

Whenever possible, incorporate kinesthetic activities in each staff development session so that, while being exposed to new knowledge, participants can move without drawing unnecessary attention to themselves, distracting others, or seeming to be rude. Activities that permit movement include acting, brainstorming, case studies, interviewing (whether simulated or real), demonstrations, role-playing, pantomime, and simulations (Dunn & Dunn, 1993; Dunn & Griggs, 1995).

In addition, consider experimenting with an interesting form of independent study, Contract Activity Packages (CAPs) (see Rose Lefkowitz's applications in Chapter 11) or Programmed Learning Sequences (PLSs) (see Roger Callan's format in Chapter 10). Both CAPs and PLSs allow participants to move while learning without disturbing others. Finally, be certain to experiment with some small-group techniques like brainstorming, circle of knowledge, group analysis, simulations, and team learning—particularly for peer-oriented adults (Dunn & Dunn, 1993; Dunn & Griggs, 1995).

THE IMPLICATIONS OF ADULTS' EMOTIONS

Motivation and Structure

Most people are motivated toward improving their skills, but some want choices of when, what, where, and with whom they will learn. Others want to be advised about what is important and how they can show that they have mastered it. Then, too, there is a range of persons on a broad, "in-between" continuum. However, if staff developers identify everyone's learning style with either the PEPS (Dunn, Dunn, & Price, 1982) or BE (Rundle & Dunn, 1996) and provide (1) variety for those who are internally structured and (2) directives for those who are externally structured, many who often verbalize their frustrations are less likely to complain. Even if they do, they will influence fewer colleagues than usual.

In addition, provide clearly printed and illustrated directions and objectives for those who need structure and alternative choices for those who do not.

Persistence

Once analytic people begin working on a task, they tend to want to finish it. Thus, analytics are less likely than globals to slip out of a workshop without closure. Global people, on the other hand, need frequent breaks. They complete tasks but feel overload when required to work straight through without intermittent snacking, taking comfort periods, or socializing (which many of them enjoy).

Either divide identified analytics and globals into two sections of the same session or acknowledge their needs and address both as best you can within the time framework and schedule.

Responsibility—Conformity versus Nonconformity

Conformists rarely pose a problem for staff developers; they'll do everything the presenter asks in exactly the way that is suggested, and if the conformists are also authority oriented, they will insist on telling the presenter that they had implemented what was described during the session.

Conversely, no matter what presenters cover or how well they plan, nonconformists will seek the other participants' and the presenter's attention by vocalizing reasons why what was suggested will not work. If they are authority oriented, they may challenge as a devil's advocate. Advise presenters to try three things when challenged by a participant: (1) explain why whatever was suggested is really important to the presenter; (2) acknowledge the person respectfully and speak in a collegial rather than an authoritative tone; and (3) provide choices for experimenting with the suggestion.

BABY STEPS TO TRY WITH ADULTS

Even the following steps should improve participants' attitudes toward, and behaviors during, staff development.

1. As each staff development session begins, on either the chalkboard, over-head transparencies, or lecture pad, the presenter should briefly make the participants aware of what they should learn during that session—their objectives. Then, as the information that the participants need to remember is introduced, they should be alerted with clues like "Be certain to write this in your notes!" or "This is important!" This type of prompting provides structure for those who need it.

2. As the material is being presented and the important information related to the session's objectives is being highlighted, the presenter should write, in large print on the chalkboard or overhead transparency, a word or phrase that synthesizes the content. That notation, particularly if accompanied by a cartoon, diagram, or drawing, will help visual learners, who will be able to "see" it while others can copy it into their notes.

3. As presenters write on that overhead transparency or lecture pad, they should illustrate important information; stick figures will do. If they cannot draw, they can ask a participant to draw it for them. Encourage global participants to illustrate their notes. Visual/analytic processors seem to respond to words and numbers; visual/global processors pay attention to drawings, symbols, and spatial designs. Both groups may profit from using colored pens, but global adults need color to attract and keep their attention. Therefore, colored chalk should be used on black-boards and colored pens should be used on overhead transparencies or white boards.

4. Strongly visual participants should be assigned a short reading to introduce new and difficult material. They then should attend the lecture or participate in a discussion of the topic. Strongly auditory participants should hear a tape or attend the session first; they then should review by reading.

   Visual participants should take—or copy—the notes the presenter is writing on the overhead transparency or chalkboard as they listen. Auditory participants should take notes while they read.

5. Experiment with turning off some lights or darkening a section of the workshop environment. Low light relaxes many global participants and permits better concentration for approximately 8 of 10 who do not enjoy reading. On the other hand, provide bright illumination in a section of the area where you are planning the professional development sessions so that analytics—and older globals—feel comfortable!

6. Write a brief illustrated outline of the presentation on either the chalk-board or on a transparency at the beginning of the session. That overview will help visual learners who cannot focus and keep track of the presenter's emphasis when only listening. Encourage presenters to draw attention to the outline from time to time and say, "Now we're moving into this part of the topic."

7. Permit alternative ways for participants to learn whatever you want them to master. Nonconforming adults (those low on the PEPS element of responsibility) thrive on options and develop positive attitudes toward learning when they are available.

~

The following chapters include many interesting and practical strategies that presenters can use during staff development to involve participants in experimenting with new ideas. Encourage presenters to try those that are most appealing to them (Raupers, 1996). We believe they will enjoy the results!

REFERENCES

Beaty, S. A. (1986). The effect of inservice training on the ability of teachers to observe learning styles of students (Doctoral dissertation, Oregon State University, 1986). *Dissertation Abstracts International, 47*, 1998A.

Buell, B. G., & Buell, N. A. (1987). Perceptual modality preference as a variable in the effectiveness of continuing education for professionals (Doctoral dissertation, University of Southern California, 1987). *Dissertation Abstracts International, 48*, 283A.

DeBello, T. (1990, July–September). Comparison of eleven major learning styles models: Variables, appropriate populations, validity of instrumentation, and the research behind them. *Journal of Reading, Writing, and Learning Disabilities International, 6*(3), 203–222.

Dunn, R., & Dunn, K. (1993). *Teaching secondary students through their individual learning styles.* Boston: Allyn & Bacon.

Dunn, R., Dunn, K., & Freeley, M. E. (1984). Tips to improve your inservice training. *Early Years, 15*(8), 43–45.

Dunn, R., Dunn, K., & Price, G. E. (1977, January). Diagnosing learning styles: A prescription for avoiding malpractice suits against school systems. *Kappan.* Indiana: Phi Delta Kappa, 418–420.

Dunn, R., Dunn, K., & Price, G. E. (1982). *Productivity Environmental Preference Survey.* Lawrence, KS: Price Systems.

Dunn, R., & Griggs, S. A. (1995). *Multiculturalism and learning styles: Teaching and counseling adolescents.* Westport, CT: Praeger.

Dunn, R., Griggs, S., Olson, J., Beasley, M., & Gorman, B. (1995). A meta-analytic validation of the Dunn and Dunn model of learning style preferences. *Journal of Educational Research, 88*(6), 353–362.

Freeley, M. E. (1984). An experimental investigation of the relationships among teachers' individual time preferences, inservice workshop schedules, and instructional techniques and the subsequent implementation of learning style strategies in participants' classrooms (Doctoral dissertation, St. John's University, 1984). *Dissertation Abstracts International, 46*, 403A.

Ingham, J. (1991). Matching instruction with employee perceptual preferences significantly increases training effectiveness. *Human Resource Development Quarterly, 2*(1), 53–64.

Marcus, L. (1977). How teachers view learning styles. *NASSP Bulletin, 61*(408), 112–114.

Raupers, P. (1996). A learning-styles approach to staff development. *Focus on Education, 40*, 38–40.

Research on the Dunn and Dunn Model. (1997). Jamaica, NY: St. John's University's Center for the Study of Learning and Teaching Styles.

Restak, R. (1979). *The brain: The last frontier.* New York: Doubleday.

Rundle, S., & Dunn, R. (1996). *Business Excellence.* Pittsford, NY: Performance Concepts, Inc.

2

Staff Development Interests and Needs: Scrambled, Poached, Fried, or Over Easy?

Jennifer Gallagher

In the technological tornado that currently engulfs America's students, most educators recognize the need for ongoing retraining and updating; yet, staff development programs for teachers are often ill-conceived, ineffectively executed, and poorly received (Wood, Thompson, & Russell, 1981). A crucial aspect of planning successful staff development programs is the process of identifying the interests and needs of the community for which the programs are intended. Common errors often occur at the very inception of ideas and topics for such programs. In order to plan a successful staff development program, several questions must be addressed:

1. Who will be involved in the assessment of needs and interests? A key issue in any planning is a carefully selected planning base. A program may encounter problems when the planning base is either too large or too small, or has conflicting interests or goals.

2. Which assessment instruments will be used to identify these needs and interests? Identification is a key issue even before the program begins; plans must be in place for assessment tools that will truly reflect the needs of the community as identified by the planning group.

3. Who will be involved in the creation and implementation of the program? As important as what the program consists of is who is selected to ·administer it; even a program with noble goals can fail if the presenter is ill prepared to "win" the audience.

4. Which resources are available for creating and implementing the program? Funding and available space are extremely important considerations in structuring programs.

5. What will be the content of the program, timetable for implementation, and intended audience or participation group? In other words, what,

when, and for whom will this program happen? These considerations can be approached creatively; perhaps educators would be well served by getting away from the "mandatory for everyone in the same way all the time" seminars.

6. Which alternatives will be available in presenting the program in response to participants' variety of learning and teaching styles? Despite the conceptual agreement among educators that people learn in different ways, staff development programs generally are designed with a traditional, auditory-based presentation method where teachers are asked to "listen" to a speaker on a given topic. Sometimes, visuals are added. Learning-styles researchers (see Dunn & Dunn, 1993) support the idea that presentations that offer alternatives for different perceptual strengths are far more effective.

7. What follow-up, evaluation, and ongoing support will be offered in order to ensure success in implementing new ideas or methods? Follow-up has been a long-neglected part of the staff development process, though there is almost universal agreement among staff development "experts" that ongoing support and follow-up are crucial to any effective staff development model (Lieberman, 1995; Fullan, 1991; Joyce & Showers, 1989; Wood et al., 1981).

Careful attention to and planning based on these seven questions can avert many of the problems which commonly sabotage staff development programs in schools. There are several models of effective staff development, including Joyce and Showers's (1989) coaching model, which address most of these questions to some degree. Necessary in a completely adequate model, however, is the idea that successful staff development changes the very culture of the school; this cultural change is difficult to accomplish in educational environments which are organized in such a way as to resist change. Also significant in its absence in staff development programs is adequate attention to the concept of teachers as learners with diverse learning styles. While most educators might conceptually agree that both children and adults process new information differently, staff development programs are to a large degree geared toward only one or two processing styles and perceptual strengths.

Effective planning for staff development, then, addresses all of the above questions *before* a program is introduced. Here is a more detailed view of the process of answering these seven questions in order to plan an effective staff development program.

First, who will be involved in the assessment of needs and interests? An important question to begin any planning session concerns who will be involved in assessing needs and planning strategies for addressing those needs. There are several key concepts to be considered here. First, a broad planning base can certainly maximize a feeling of ownership among the participants in a program and generally leads to less resistance to new ideas. If an administrator or group of administrators identifies a need and plans a program to address that need, teachers, parents, and students may feel that they have no voice in changing the school climate and may therefore resist a program despite its merit. An unfortunate example of this type of resistance occurred in New York City in the late 1980s, when Chancellor Joseph Fernandez attempted to implement the "Rainbow Curriculum." Had Fernandez begun with a broader planning base, he may have been able to forestall some of the objections or arrive at a compromise that would have allowed him to introduce a curriculum on diversity without the furor among parents and community groups that ensued during that time.

On the other hand, the larger the planning base, the "messier" the process may be; democracy was never intended to be the most efficient form of government. A large planning base may include groups with diverse interests and perspectives, and it may be more challenging and time consuming to bring these groups to consensus on the needs of the school community. While the large size and diversity of a planning group may slow the planning process, these characteristics may also alleviate any resistance to the program later on, thus increasing the overall effectiveness of the program.

A key consideration for an administrator or staff development planner is the desired outcome and necessity of the program. If the need is immediate and clear and requires prompt attention, it may not be necessary to use a large planning group. Most staff development programs, however, are based on long-term, complex needs. For these needs a larger planning base is generally better. The administrator's roles in this type of planning process would be to recruit a dynamic facilitator and to design a process by which the perspectives of all groups can be heard within a reasonable timetable. That is no small task!

It is, therefore, necessary to move to our second question: Which assessment instruments will be used to identify these needs and interests? Once a decision is made regarding the composition of the planning group, it is necessary to design an effective approach for assessing and evaluating needs. If one merely asks each group's representative to specify an appropriate staff development program, each group will likely offer its own narrow focus or perspective, perhaps without an awareness of the broader picture. This type of brainstorming might be an effective starting point for needs assessment, but it would be important to have a structure in place for evaluating these needs with respect to their importance to the entire educational community. For example, the following is a hypothetical list of possible staff development topics surfaced by an imaginary group of administrators, teachers, parents, and community leaders:

1. interdisciplinary teaching
2. teaching students through their individual learning styles
3. alternative assessment methods
4. conflict resolution strategies
5. cooperative learning strategies

6. writing across the curriculum

7. dealing with at-risk students

After each group has identified the topics or needs that they wish to be addressed, it would be appropriate to give some time to discussing why each of these topics would be important to the school community. This discussion could be accomplished in small heterogeneous groups, with each group reporting back to the larger group the three topics they would give top priority too. A smaller committee or an administrator could be responsible for the final selection of a topic or topics for staff development. This type of process allows everyone to have a voice and also fosters discussion on the wide range of needs in the educational community served by the group.

The next logical step would involve planning the actual implementation and content of the staff development program. Once again, it is important to determine: Who will be involved in the creation and implementation of the program? The group that will actually create and implement a staff development program might be composed of representatives from the larger needs assessment group and might also include others who were not part of the original group, but who have some expertise in this area. This group needs to be smaller than the original group, since this group will focus on a more specific task. The exact number and composition of this group can be determined by the facilitators/administrators after they consider the type of program that will be offered. If the group opts to have the program created and/or implemented primarily by an outside source, it is of vital importance that the presenter/program director be someone who is well equipped to conduct the program. Too often staff developers are booked on the basis of word-of-mouth recommendations, not as a result of thorough firsthand research and investigation.

Another key consideration in planning staff development programs involves answering the question: Which resources are available for creating and implementing the program? The answers to this question determine what is possible and realistic in creating any new program. Funding, space, and time constraints are fundamental considerations; they need not, however, be insurmountable obstacles. Joyce and Showers (1989), for example, have published some low-cost arrangements for implementing their coaching method, and creative administrators and teachers can find other ways to implement programs within a given budget. The same is true for time and space constraints; realism is important in deciding which approach to take, but creativity is important in maximizing the use of available resources.

Once it is determined which resources are available, and what the focus of the program should be, it is necessary to determine: What will be the content of the program, timetable for implementation, and intended audience or participation group? These are perhaps the most important considerations in staff development planning because they refer to the very heart of what the staff development program will do. Once needs assessments are completed, priorities are articulated, and resources are analyzed, it is necessary to decide the actual content of the program, the implementation process and timetable, and intended audience or participation group. Ann Lieberman (1995) suggests some radical rethinking in these areas to create a "culture of inquiry" among professional educators. Lieberman recommends the creation of new staff development structures, such as problem-solving groups and decision-making teams, which would create an infrastructure for ongoing staff development within each school community. Others, such as Joyce and Showers (1982), have long advocated new roles among educators (e.g., peer coaches and teacher leaders) to facilitate the process of staff development. There is, however, no structure, role, or staff development program which is perfect for every school, every district, or every teacher for that matter! Critical in determining the content and process of a program for a particular community is a full analysis of the needs of that particular school or district. What works in an affluent community might very well be superfluous in an inner-city system; what is most needed for a small private preschool might be very different from what is most needed for a large public high school in the same geographic area.

Some paradigms can exist for the creation of staff development programs, then, but the actual content and implementation of each program must be based on the individual needs of each educational community.

In analyzing the best way to implement a staff development program for a given community, it is necessary to take into account: Which alternatives are available in presenting the program in response to participants' variety of learning and teaching styles? Despite research that supports the idea that instruction is more effective when it is approached through the learner's perceptual and processing strengths (Dunn & Dunn, 1993), staff development programs are generally structured with little attention to the variety of learning and teaching styles of the audience. The traditional after-school staff development workshop is probably best for analytics with auditory and late-afternoon learning preferences; this is actually a very small percentage of the population. Most of the teachers who attend staff development programs, then, are probably not being served very well. A truly creative staff developer could design programs with a variety of options geared toward the learning styles of the audience. Stories, songs, and jokes could be structured into a presentation to appeal to the global thinkers in the audience. Videotapes of the presentation could be made for those whose time-of-day preference makes late-afternoon learning difficult. Visual aids, manipulatives (for tactual learners), group activities, and opportunities for mobility (for kinesthetics) are some other options that could easily be structured into presentations in order to better capitalize on the learning strengths of the audience.

In addition, perhaps the best way to address the learning- and teaching-style diversity of teachers is to move away from staff development workshops entirely. Learning is a complex and dynamic process; few teachers would expect their students to learn and use new concepts on the basis of one lesson. That is, however, exactly what we expect teachers to do when they attend staff development workshops.

Many specialists in staff development have suggested that one of the most critical components of staff development is ongoing support and follow-up (Lieberman, 1995; Fullan, 1991; Rogers, 1987; Joyce & Showers, 1982). The final question to address in planning a staff development program, then, is: What follow-up, evaluation, and ongoing support will be offered in order to ensure success in implementing new ideas or methods?

There are many methods of support and evaluation that are possible and effective for staff development programs. What is essential, however, is that some type of follow-up is implemented. Ongoing support is built into several effective models of staff development, including Joyce and Showers's (1982) coaching method. Follow-up in this model is accomplished through the continuing relationship between coach and teacher wherein both evaluate and analyze strategies and responses. Sandra Rogers (1987) suggests the use of videotapes in the evaluation process. These allow the teacher to see what actually happened in the classroom, rather than what he or she *thought* happened. Ann Lieberman suggests the creation of a culture of inquiry, similar to that suggested by Michael Fullan (1991), where ongoing evaluation of staff development is a part of the very nature of the educational community.

Other possibilities for ongoing support include conferences with follow-up meetings at a later date, the involvement of staff development trainers who can actually work with teachers in the classroom in implementing strategies, and evaluation processes with several parts and timetables. Some sort of follow-up is possible and essential in every staff development offering.

If there is a governing principle to be used in planning staff development programs, it is definitely flexibility. Those responsible for staff development can follow some guidelines for effective planning, such as the seven questions outlined in this chapter, but more important is the adaptation of these guidelines to a particular situation. The failure of staff development programs has been in their relative uniformity and lack of creativity. When we begin to plan programs for teachers using the same principles that we use for students, we will see a new type of staff development emerge that more closely resembles the culture of inquiry suggested by Ann Lieberman (1995). Despite the fact that learning is among the most dynamic and least understood of human processes, education—the process of learning—has remained relatively static in its development across time and particularly during this century. The creation of a dynamic staff development climate for teachers might well be an important step in the further development of that same type of climate for our students. Perhaps by enacting some of the ideas discussed here, school personnel can truly create a successful recipe for community participation in staff development planning.

REFERENCES

Dunn, R., & Dunn, K. (1993). *Teaching secondary students through their individual learning styles.* Boston: Allyn & Bacon.

Fullan, M. (Ed.). (1991). *Staff development, innovation, and institutional development: Changing school culture through staff development.* Alexandria, VA: Association for Supervision and Curriculum Development.

Joyce, B. & Showers, B. (1982). Coaching of teaching. *Educational Leadership, 40*(1), 4–10.

Joyce, B. & Showers, B. (1989). School renewal as cultural change. *Educational Leadership, 47*(3), 70–77.

Lieberman, A. (1995). Practices that support teacher development. *Phi Delta Kappan, 76*(8), 591–596.

Rogers, S. (1987, October). If I can see myself, I can change. *Educational Leadership,* 64–67.

Wood, F., Thompson, S., & Russell, F. (1981). Designing effective staff development programs. Staff development/organization development. Alexandria, VA: Association for Supervision and Curriculum Development.

3

Incentives for Staff Development: "Brother, Can You Spare the Time?"

Fran Guastello and Anita Sobol

In recent years, teachers have been more involved in the decision-making process in the critical areas of improved teaching and learning, curriculum development, and school organization. These additional responsibilities necessitate supportive and ongoing staff development. What can be done to motivate a faculty to accept leadership roles in contributing to the improvement of instruction?

> *This is Ms. Thompson's first year as an intermediate school teacher. The entire school is working on developing portfolio assessment. Although she is familiar with the term, she has had very little experience assessing students in this capacity. She's somewhat hesitant to become involved in this process. However, the fact that she can attend off-site seminars at Crossroads School every Thursday morning has enabled her to participate in the planning and implementation with much more confidence and enthusiasm. Mr. Hoffman has already worked on a similar project so he was thrilled to have the opportunity to be the guest speaker at I.S. 73 to deliver the first of several workshops on this topic.*
>
> *Mr. Smith has been teaching social studies in the same school as Ms. Thompson for 22 years. He did not attend the seminar, for, as he remarked to the principal at the faculty meeting, "We tried that idea 11 years ago, Al, and it didn't work then either. I'm just not going to do it."*

In almost every school environment there are varying levels of experience and attitudes. Strategies that are individual and yet all-encompassing should be used to motivate staff to begin, participate, and persist in a new program. This chapter will suggest techniques and incentives that will motivate most teachers to embrace programs that promise improved learning, better student attitudes, and fewer discipline problems.

MOTIVATION

*"Have you seen the flyers for this year's staff development workshops?" John Ames
could not contain his enthusiasm and astonishment. "Not only do these topics
reflect what we asked for in the needs assessment, but Ms. McGuire has really
made them enticing." "Look at this, John," exclaimed Mrs. Henderson. "Working with my students on this fine arts project will enable me to take that
calligraphy course I've always wanted to enroll in at St. John's. This is great!"
"Being able to use one of the school computers at my home over the summer will
certainly allow me the opportunity to learn the program and help my students
with computer-assisted instruction on reading next fall," echoes Ms. Katelin.*

An integral aspect of effective staff development is motivation. Needs assessments provide us with the content to be addressed in developing programs to meet
the needs of the staff. But the more challenging task is to motivate individuals to
participate, contribute, and persist in their efforts to learn and improve the quality
of teaching.

Human Needs

Individuals need caring leaders who address their immediate human needs as a
strategy to begin the process of long-term professional growth. If we can make a
positive difference in the lives of educators, we will improve the lives of children
and the adults that they influence (McCarty, 1993). When individuals have high
self-esteem they are likely to behave in purposeful, motivated, productive, cooperative, and creative ways (Coopersmith, 1967; Reasoner, 1991). The following nine
areas, as outlined by McCarty (1993), provide opportunities to change the psychological environment of a school and increase positive innovation, change, and
growth:

1. safety: creating an atmosphere where teachers feel free from fear of
   physical, sexual, emotional, and social abuse
2. identity: making each staff member feel special or unique and recognizing
   special accomplishments
3. connectedness: creating a feeling of affection, inclusion, and affiliation
   among the staff
4. power: "needs and opinions reflected in the policies of the school and of
   the district" (Maeroff, 1988, p. 32)
5. meaningfulness: making one feel that life is purposeful
6. risk taking: minimizing the fear of risk by offering special training and
   taking small steps
7. models and mentors schedule professional sessions with the right people
8. counseling: providing it, if needed

9. fun: helping us relax and giving us a "sense of perspective," a context into which to put all the events of our personal and professional lives.

Incentives

Whenever possible, tailor incentives for participants. Needs assessments might include questions about incentives as part of the assessment. When providing topics for staff development which have resulted from questionnaires or meetings, ask the teachers, "Which incentives would encourage you to participate and implement the programs to be initiated?" In other words, ask them to create a "wish list" for the project. Responses to these questions should provide some direction for the types of incentives that would be motivating and beneficial to the staff. In addition, ask the staff to create a list of incentives and to rank them in order of value.

Here is a sample:

What incentives might encourage you to implement this program or these techniques in your classroom/school?

___ I'd like to visit a school where students are actually using this program to see how it is implemented.

___ I'd need a course in basic computer skills to feel confident enough to help my students.

___ I'd like to be able to develop my own incentives.

___ I'd like to be able to establish a link with a person in another school who is using this program in case I need some assistance.

___ I'd like a program of coaching established with

   ___ An administrator

   ___ Peers

   ___ A qualified consultant

   ___ College professors

   ___ Other

___ I'd like to have the staff agree to an incentive point program for students with rewards. For example:

When all of your students have reached a combined total of 10,000 points, your principal will take you to lunch!

When they've reached 25,000 points, your principal will pay for a mini-course of your choice.

That which motivates or reinforces is as unique as each teacher's individual learning style. Thus staff development sessions are more stimulating, instructive, and exciting when the participants' environmental, emotional, sociological, physical, and psychological needs are met (see Chapter 1). Incentives that entice teachers are just as individualistic. Which factors have potential incentive value? Try this questionnaire. Have the staff add, modify, or create their own.

Personal Reinforcement Checklist

Directions: Below are a group of activities that you may or may not enjoy. Please add any activities that you feel are highly rewarding or motivating to you. Rate them by circling the appropriate number for each activity.

	Reinforcement Value				
	1	2	3	4	5
	Low		Mid		High
1. Eating					
Ice cream	1	2	3	4	5
Carrots	1	2	3	4	5
Bread	1	2	3	4	5
Peanuts	1	2	3	4	5
Fruit	1	2	3	4	5
Coffee	1	2	3	4	5
Rolls	1	2	3	4	5
Other_____	1	2	3	4	5
2. Reading					
Books	1	2	3	4	5
Reference materials	1	2	3	4	5
Magazines	1	2	3	4	5
Other_____	1	2	3	4	5
3. Hobbies and crafts					
Gardening	1	2	3	4	5
Sewing	1	2	3	4	5
Automobiles	1	2	3	4	5
Other_____	1	2	3	4	5
4. General activities					
Traveling	1	2	3	4	5
Parties	1	2	3	4	5
Dancing	1	2	3	4	5
Playing games	1	2	3	4	5
Attending religious service	1	2	3	4	5
Exercising	1	2	3	4	5
Meditating	1	2	3	4	5
Meeting new people	1	2	3	4	5
Receiving compliments	1	2	3	4	5
Being recognized by name	1	2	3	4	5
Other_____	1	2	3	4	5

TYPES OF INCENTIVES AND REWARDS

Incentives can be personal or social:

- special recognition from administrators, district leaders, peers, parents, or students, for example, awards, letters of recognition, bulletin board display
- public recognition, for example, newspaper or magazine articles, TV commercials, radio or phone messages broadcasted
- certificates of recognition
- promotion to team leader or coordinator
- slection as teacher of the week/month/year
- invitation to be a guest speaker
- luncheon or dinner to honor one's accomplishment
- mental challenges
- autonomy
- personal feelings of achievement, accomplishment, and satisfaction
- personal commitment to learning and continuous improvement

Incentives can be materialistic:

- inexpensive tokens, for example, T-shirt, name plate for desk, business cards
- items for the teacher's classroom that he or she has always wanted
- cash allowance to buy materials for the classroom
- gift certificate
- merit pay/bonus
- grant
- opportunity to attend an all-expenses-paid conference of choice
- membership for one year in a health club
- library acquisitions
- computer access
- an extra excused personal day off
- an extra prep period for one semester
- one free college course
- leadership role with title
- co-authorship of a book
- promotion and professional advancement

POSSIBLE SOURCES OF ASSISTANCE

Surveying the list above, you will note that most rewards need not be costly; many are of intrinsic value which meet the needs of the individual. Even the extrinsic or materialistic rewards cost little and often can be obtained from private organizations, schools, or educational research foundations. Some suggested funding sources are:

- general categorical funds which are made to a district for a specific reason but which can be spent on any district function
- matching grants from private foundations
- parents' associations
- private industry
- fund-raising activities
- alumni associations
- colleges and universities
- research and development agencies

CONCLUSION

Incentives have proven to be highly motivating as a strategy because they can be designed to meet the unique needs and characteristics of each staff member. Further, the wide range of incentives that could be offered can realistically be designed within the structures of a modest budget. There is no doubt that motivational strategies such as incentives will improve and enhance participation and persistence in achieving staff development goals. Teachers who believe that administrators, parents, other teachers, and school board members care and are willing to provide meaningful recognition, growth opportunities, desired rewards, and opportunities to succeed and to accomplish objectives will join a productive staff development program with great enthusiasm.

REFERENCES

Appelbaum, E., & Batt, R. (1993). American models of high performance work systems. *AFL-CIO Department of Economic Research, 3,* 67–100.

Capelli, P., & Iannozzi, M. (1993). Challenge: To develop incentives for investment in educational workforce. *EQW Issue, 5,* 2–9.

Carter, M., & Powell, D. (1992). Teacher leaders as staff developers. *Journal of Staff Development, 13*(1), 8–12.

Chait, R. (1994). Make us an offer. *Trusteeship, 2,* 28–34.

Chapman, D. W., Snyder, C. W., & Burchfield, S. A. (1993). Teacher incentives in the third world. *Teacher & Teacher Education, 9,* 301–316.

Coopersmith, S. (1967). *Antecedents of self-esteem.* San Francisco, CA: W. Freeman.

Dunn, R., & Dunn, K. (1993). *Teaching secondary students through their individual learning styles: Practical approaches for grades 7–12.* Needham Heights, MA: Allyn and Bacon.

Farmer, D. (1993). Designing a reward system to promote the career development of senior faculty. *New Directions in Teaching and Learning, 55,* 43–53.

Froh, R. C., Menges, R. J. & Walker, C. J. (1993). Revitalizing faculty work through intrinsic rewards. *New Directions for Higher Education, 81,* 87–95.

Glaser, W. (1984). *Control theory: A new explanation of how we control our lives.* New York: Harper and Row.

Kearney, S. (1994). Success, Inc.: Tips for a local educational foundation: Funding for the future. *Delta Kappa Gamma Bulletin, 61*(1), 11–60.

Kluepitel, G., Parelius, R. J., & Ruberts, G. (1994). Involving faculty in retention. *Journal of Developmental Education, 17,* 16–18, 20, 22, 24, 26.

Kostoff, R. N, Averch, H. A., & Chubin, D. E. (1994). Research, impact assessment: Introduction & overview. *Evaluation Review, 18,* 3–10.

Lonsdale, A. (1993). Changes in incentives, rewards and sanctions. *Higher Education Management, 5,* 223–236.

Maeroff, G. I. (1988). A blueprint for empowering teachers. *Phi Delta Kappan, 69*(7), 472–477.

McCarty, H. (1991). *Self-esteem: The bottom line in school success.* Sacramento, CA: Learning Resource Publishers.

McCarty, H. (1993). From deadwood to greenwood: Working with burned out staff. *Journal of Staff Development, 14*(1), 42–46.

McKenzie, J. F., Luebke, J. K., & Romas, J. A. (1992). Incentives: Getting & keeping workers involved in health promotion programs. *Journal of Health Education, 23,* 70–73.

Moseley, M. (1992). Educating faculty for teaching in an interdisciplinary general education sequence. *Journal of General Education, 41,* 8–17.

Picus, L. (1991). Incentive funding programs and school district response: California and Senate Bill 813. *Educational Evaluation and Policy Analysis, 13*(3), 289–308.

Price, J. (1994). The school administrator supply and demand report. *Wisconsin Department of Public Instruction,* 1–26.

Reasoner, R. W. (1991). *Building self-esteem in the secondary schools: Teacher's manual.* Palo Alto, CA: Consulting Psychologists Press.

Sparks, D., & Vaugn, S. (1994). What every school board member should know about staff development. *Journal of Staff Development, 15*(2), 20–22.

Younger, S. M. (1993). Four by four: Finding time for TQM training. *Training & Development, 15,* 11–15.

4

Informal Forms of Staff Development: Cushion the Task!

Daniel T. Arcieri

Very much like third graders, university freshmen, and even laboratory rodents, adult learners have distinct needs when it comes to learning. According to recent research, adults learn much more effectively through active participation and by studying through their learning-style strengths than they do through passive listening. Generally speaking, many adults also are competency-based learners, meaning that they want to acquire practical knowledge or skills that they can use in their immediate environment. Unfortunately, much of staff development, like much of conventional teaching, is often packaged in a lecture format in which participants are merely passive recipients. Such staff development is formal in both design and presentation and assumes that workshops and seminars are just transferable packages of information to be distributed among personnel. By their willingness to grant credit to the participants, administrators imply that employing consultants *outside* the school counts, whereas opportunities to learn with and from colleagues *inside* the school do not.

However, if conventional staff development, which is so widely practiced, is a solution to performance problems, why do such programs rarely match the participants' expectations? And why are staff so reluctant to attend them? Why is staff development often deemed irrelevant to the workplace and, ultimately, why have consistent staff development programs been unable to remedy the persistent problems that exist? Honesty suggests that formal staff development is weak in both content and presentation when compared with the continuing professional learning that normally is fostered inside an organization when its personnel are aware of what to do.

The power of professional development increases dramatically when it is viewed as an integral part of the organization's existence. Multiple forms of job-embedded learning help create a culture of inquiry where learning and development are expected, sought, and promoted as an ongoing aspect of working among professional people. What characterizes these informal learning practices is that they last not for two hours or two days but, rather, for each professional's lifetime.

What are these new opportunities for, and broader conceptions of, professional development, and how can they be built into the activities of each day? This chapter provides a few answers.

KICK-START YOUR CREATIVITY!

Of course your organization has problems; every group has. However, that does not necessarily mean that you need to employ an outside consultant to generate creative solutions. How can you and your colleagues increase the level of innovation so as to solve ongoing problems? Here are a few ways to help your colleagues create creativity.

- *Once a week:* Have all staff members meet at a designated time and place each week to rethink or reorganize only one area of work. At the end of that week, those who attended the meeting and experimented with suggested changes during the remainder of that week should meet again for just 10 minutes to share what each did differently and how it worked for that individual.

- *Two ways:* Do not entertain a single negative comment concerning a new idea or proposal. Ask people in self-selected pairs to think of at least two ways to implement one new or suggested idea before it may be rejected. They then need to try it—and report back to the group in 10 minutes at the same time and place the following week.

- *Change places:* Ask each employee, supervisor, and any other person to spend at least part of a work day in another department. After they have done so, have department heads meet with them informally to obtain their perceptions. The visitors should be asked what they would do differently if they worked in those departments, and why. Consider their thoughts soberly.

- *Brainstorming board:* Write a problem or concern on a large sheet of paper and place it at the top of a bulletin board which is on a wall in a central location. Make a small paper pad available so that ideas or solutions can be written and posted onto the board. Read them.

- *"Do" lunch:* Invite all organizational employees to attend weekly lunch meetings to discuss current problems and to generate creative solutions. Invite administrators and supervisors to participate.

- *Creativity committee:* An idea-generating group can be formed from members of different departments. This committee can be charged with eliciting, discussing, and implementing ideas provided by employees that they believe have promise. An incentive system might be designed to reward quality contributions.

TRY NEW ROLES AND STRUCTURES

If professionals are to change the way they work, they must be provided with viable opportunities to discuss and experiment with new practices. For example, teachers need to learn about, develop, and use new ideas in and out of their classrooms. Here are a number of suggestions:

- Develop new roles such as teacher-leader, teacher-researcher, and peer-coach. These broader responsibilities can generate a deeper understanding of teaching methodology and learning theory.
- Create new organizational structures like creative problem-solving committees and decision-making teams. Many individuals prefer to work with others and work better that way than they do alone. It's just their learning style.
- Work on new tasks as a small, interested unit. Tasks can include such varied directions as learning how to evaluate how well each person contributes to the organization's stated goals or identifying staff members' learning styles as a way of interacting better with each other. The unit should periodically report back to peers either formally or informally—but planned feedback must be included in the process.

TRY NEW APPROACHES

Experimentation with, or adoption of, innovative approaches can provide incentive for many professionals. Trying something original to determine its effectiveness often provides a personal challenge that leads to real growth. Here are two approaches that capitalize on students' and teachers' abilities to stimulate learning.

- The Foxfire approach encourages educators to use students' interests and aptitudes to involve them in the design and execution of their own lessons. Students gain skills and knowledge as they write, edit, and produce work in subjects that attract them. The Foxfire approach progresses from encouraging students to choose their own topics to research and write about, to involving them in identifying their own learning traits as their teachers serve as guides.
- Whole-language approaches to integrating the language arts can involve teachers and students in planning blocks of time to read, write, listen, and speak. Experimenting with this approach involves educators in the same struggle for intellectual growth as their students.

IDENTIFY ADULTS' INDIVIDUAL LEARNING STYLES

Through observations and the use of the Dunn, Dunn, and Price Learning Styles Inventory, teachers can expand their understanding of what is truly possible in today's schools. This giant leap will only occur when they become aware of, and plan for, differences in how each of their many students learns. The goal here is to focus on both students' strengths and needs so that teachers can develop more effective strategies for classroom use. Understanding learning styles also allows teachers to teach students to teach themselves by capitalizing on personal strengths. When students were taught through their identified learning styles, they experienced a statistically significant increase in academic achievement, developed improved attitudes toward instruction, and caused fewer discipline problems than when they were taught through their nonpreferred styles (Dunn & Dunn, 1993).

Similarly, identifying each adult's learning style with either the Productivity Environmental Preference Survey (Dunn, Dunn, & Price, 1982) or Business Excellence (Rundle & Dunn, 1996) will increase your colleagues' appreciation of the differences that exist among themselves. It will also generate their interest in learning how to interpret their own, their spouse's, their offsprings', and their students' learning styles. It's only a small step from becoming aware of the differences among learning styles to wanting to learn how to make the appropriate environmental and instructional changes to address those differences. Invariably, increased professionalism results, as well as at least some positive and permanent change in the lives of both students and teachers.

LEARNING OUTSIDE STAFF DEVELOPMENT SESSIONS

We all agree that school is a great place to learn. But growing evidence suggests that important and powerful opportunities for professional learning can be found outside the school environment too. Unique arrangements such as coalitions, collaborations, and networks offer alternatives to staff development programs and other more traditional forms of staff training. By getting involved in informal groups, educators can experience learning in comfortable environments, gain confidence in themselves, and contribute to a shared understanding that leads to intellectual development. You get all of this while learning exactly what you want to learn and at your own pace. Here are some examples.

The International Learning Styles Network

This network has been cosponsored by the National Association of Secondary School Principals and St. John's University (New York) since 1979. Its purpose is to support and encourage teachers as they pursue learning-styles techniques and approaches. The network currently includes 17 regional centers in the United States and abroad and also publishes a newsletter that translates cutting-edge research into practical how-to steps. Reports of how these practices work in geographically diverse schools are also available. Other services include information about conferences, institutes, and staff development workshops for teachers and administrators; descriptions of publications and dissertations in the field; identification of resource personnel and exemplary school sites; an updated bibliography of publications and films; and responses to written or telephone requests for information. For information or an application to join, write to: Professor Rita Dunn, Learning Styles Network, St. John's University, Utopia Parkway, Jamaica, New York 11439.

The Foxfire Outreach Network

One teacher's strategy for allowing students to choose areas of interest to pursue as part of their lesson plan expanded to the founding of 20 groups across the United States. Knowing that meaningful and lasting learning must be supported continuously, the Foxfire Outreach Network attempts to provide professional development for teachers who use this approach. Teachers help teachers translate new concepts into worthwhile classroom activities. From theory to practice, all levels of understanding are investigated.

AVOID RESISTANCE

The list of changes occurring in and out of formal professional development that have affected how we function is endless. Change has become an everyday part of organizational life. Having employees resist change can be a fundamental problem with respect to necessary professional growth. Resistance to change can become a problem so huge that it could cripple an entire organization. What are the symptoms and causes of resistance and some of the possible remedies? Here are some of the adult behaviors and verbalizations you need to note before you effectively will be able to implement new ideas. Be alert for the people who

- agree verbally, but rarely follow through
- procrastinate
- feign ignorance
- withhold support, help, or suggestions
- are openly critical to prevent others from trying
- sabotage
- block
- threaten or intimidate

The reasons behind their behaviors may include

- a lack of motivation because they perceive that things are acceptable the way they are
- a view of change as a threat rather than as an advantage
- mishandling by management of the change process
- the belief that the change will fail
- the belief that the proposed change is too radical or rapid
- a top-down approach to change that is offensive to the employees' sense of autonomy and integrity
- inattention to the learning styles of staff

Here are some suggested remedies:

- Show the need for the change. People who cannot find a good reason for change are more likely to resist.
- Stress objectives and identify goals.
- Maintain enthusiasm; it is the fuel for maintaining interest in change.
- Provide feedback that reinforces; give credit and recognition to motivate learners.
- Include *all* professionals in the planning and implementation process.
- Capitalize on your colleagues' learning styles whenever possible.

PROFESSIONALS NEED TO CONSTANTLY UPGRADE THEIR SKILLS

All members of the school community must see themselves as staff developers. Job-embedded professional learning means that teachers and other important stakeholders become integral parts of designing and implementing both informal and conventional forms of professional growth. To meet future challenges all those who affect students' learning—administrators, teachers, and professional staff— need to continually upgrade their knowledge and skills. Thus, including varied groups in the planning and execution of staff development is likely to

- reduce resistance
- foster a cohesive, collaborative environment. Research suggests that there is a strong positive correlation between employees' participation and their commitment to change.
- provide a variety of perspectives necessary to accurately determine if a specific problem is performance related or organizational
- elevate the self-esteem of the varied participants
- continually promote informal forms of staff improvement

REFERENCES

Allen, B. (1994, December). A case study in planning staff development: What do teachers really want? *American Annals of the Deaf, 139*(5), 493–499.

Assayesh, G. (1994). Effective advocacy for staff development. *Journal of Staff Development, 15*(1), 52–55.

Dunn, K., Dunn, R., & Freeley, M. (1985, April). Tips to improve your in-service training: Knowing *your* learning style. *Early Years: K-8, 15*(8), 30–31.

Dunn, R., & Dunn, K. (1993). *Teaching secondary students through their individual learning styles.* Boston: Allyn and Bacon.

Dunn, R., Dunn, K., & Price, G. E. (1982). *Productivity Environmental Preference Survey.* Lawrence, KS: Price Systems.

Higgins, J. (1994). Creating creativity. *Training and Development, 48*(1), 11–15.

Hultman, K. (1995, October). Scaling the wall of resistance. *Training and Development, 32*(10), 34–37.

Leggett, D., & Hoyle, S. (1987). Peer coaching: One district's experience in using teachers as staff developers. *Journal of Staff Development, 8*(1), 16–20.

Lieberman, A. (1995). Practices that support teacher development. *Phi Delta Kappan, 76*(8), 591–596.

Michalko, M. (1994). Bright ideas. *Training and Development, 48*(6), 44–47.

Rundle, S., & Dunn, R. (1996). *Business excellence.* Pittsford, NY: Performance Concepts, Inc.

Tallerico, K. (1987). Building level staff development: A personal account of peers helping peers. *Journal of Staff Development, 8*(1), 32–34.

Zemke, R., & Zemke, S. (1995, June). Adult learning: What do we know for sure? *Training, 32*(6), 31–40.

5

Technology:
The Latest Line of Learning-Style Tools

Patricia M. Raupers and Patrice H. Roberts

Helen and Mary are excellent teachers by all existing measures. They are dedicated professionals who use a learning-style approach in their classrooms. Both are committed to becoming as professional as possible. They are involved in numerous professional development activities and they frequently collaborate with other teachers. However, Helen and Mary are at opposite ends of a continuum concerning their attitudes about the use of technology in their classrooms.

Helen is computer literate and experiments with technology as an instructional resource. She frequently "surfs the Net" in search of new ideas for teaching. She is eager to attend staff development programs on technological topics. Helen believes that technology can provide her with tools to help her individualize instruction for her students.

Mary is terrified by technology; she has only recently figured out how to stop the blinking on her VCR! She suspects that she might break the equipment if she uses it and that her lessons will fail if she relies on technological components—because "with media, something always goes wrong!" Mary feels secure with traditional individualized resources.

Staff developers can help Helen and Mary and all the people in between when they develop programs that address the learning-style preferences of the participants they are trying to reach. Modifications can be made to conventional instructional programs with a minimal amount of time and effort. Such modifications can lead to an environment that encourages everyone—teachers and students—to make the most of the opportunity to learn. As Ingham (1991) found, when the learning-style preferences of adult learners were identified and responded to during the training, statistically higher achievement and attitude gains were made than when they were not. In addition, when staff developers adjust the training experience, it serves as a powerful model for teachers who need to meet the diverse learning styles of their students.

RESPONDING TO STUDENTS' STYLES WITH TECHNOLOGY TRAINING

"Learning style is the way in which individuals begin to concentrate on, process, internalize, and retain new and difficult academic information" (Dunn, Griggs, Olson, Beasley, & Gorman, 1995, p. 353). Because they want all students to succeed, teachers plan for diverse learners. To some extent, teachers respond to students' uniqueness when they deliver instruction in a variety of ways, provide options, and use varied assessments (Association for Supervision and Curriculum Development, 1992). Indeed, educators have been developing instructional strategies, multisensory resources, and thematic units of instruction to accommodate students' different styles for years.

Technology adds new tools to teachers' strategies as they try to respond to individuals' many learning styles. For example, a Programmed Learning Sequence (PLS) (see Chapter 10) can be created on the computer for those students who prefer to work alone and need to avoid the sounds and distractions caused by classmates. PLSs often appeal to visual learners and those in need of structure (Dunn & Dunn, 1993). PLSs are available in both hard copy and on disk. However, because of their different learning styles, some teachers—and some students—will be comfortable using a PLS on the computer and delight in its potential for animated and interactive programs, whereas other teachers—and students—will prefer the PLS printed-book format and become intensely involved in manipulating the tactual electroboards, task cards, or pic-a-holes that are built into its frames (see Chapter 12).

Teachers—and students—who are motivated to use computers can create their own Contract Activity Packages (CAPs) (see Chapter 11). "Teachers who believe that the greatest gifts they can give to their students are a love of learning and the tools to teach themselves easily will enjoy the effects of contracting" (Dunn & Dunn, 1993, p. 273). The computer is an effective resource to promote independent learning in school. In addition, when teachers have trouble reaching students, or when students have trouble understanding what their teacher is trying to teach, a supplementary computer program that introduces the concept or skill in another way—one that matches the student's learning style—may be just the answer (Vockell & Mihail, 1993). It is important to remember that difficulty while learning may not relate to the content, but rather to the mismatch between the instructional delivery and the students' learning style.

After teachers have become fairly comfortable with word processing, the Internet, multimedia, and presentation programs such as Hyperstudio and Power Point, they need to begin a more advanced program. Staff developers can help teachers make connections between technological tools and their desire to respond to their students' learning styles. Teachers need to apply the knowledge and skills they have gained to the creation of resources and strategies to enhance their students' higher-level thinking and independent learning in new, effective patterns.

Although "technology can individualize instruction" (Peck & Dorricott, 1994, p. 12), if teachers' learning-style preferences are not addressed in their own training experiences, they will be unable to fully internalize and use what they have learned.

Therefore, the full promise of classroom technological adaptation may not be realized. Learning-style strategies are central to every stage of a staff development program.

DESIGNING PROFESSIONAL DEVELOPMENT PROGRAMS IN TECHNOLOGY TO ACCOMMODATE PARTICIPANTS' LEARNING-STYLE PREFERENCES

Prior to training teachers to use technology as one of the strategies for the individualization of instruction, staff developers need to either identify the participants' learning styles or plan for varied learning-style opportunities to accommodate expected learning-style preferences. Knowledge of the Dunn and Dunn Learning Styles Model (Dunn & Dunn, 1993) can assist staff developers as they attempt to address the environmental, emotional, sociological, physiological, and psychological preferences of the participants.

The Dunn and Dunn model is based on sound theoretical assumptions. Learning style is a biological and developmental collection of personal characteristics—which causes the same instructional environments, methods, and resources to be effective with some learners and ineffective with others. All people have learning-style preferences, but individuals in the same workshop are likely to have extremely different preferences. When participants learn about technology, which may be new and difficult for some, it is important that they each experience instructional strategies that complement their special styles—or they may turn off to computers without ever having turned one on. Not only does accommodating learning-style preferences increase understanding of new information, it also improves participants' attitudes toward professional development (Griggs, Griggs, Dunn, & Ingham, 1994).

Responding to Participants' Environmental Preferences

Environmental preferences for sound, light, temperature, and design can be readily addressed. Sound can be accommodated by volume adjustment and the use of speakers, earphones, microphones, sound cards, and, in some cases, ear plugs to obtain silence. By adjusting contrast, using a screen filter, manipulating color on a monitor, or moving a laptop to bright or soft illumination, staff developers can meet different light preferences. Since some learners prefer warm—whereas other learners prefer cool—temperatures when learning new and difficult information, the use of laptop computers enables them to relocate to a comfortable environment. Three accommodations for design preferences are the use of (1) formal stations with desktop computers, (2) laptop computers in an informal setting, and (3) LCD panels to project onto a large surface to allow seating design choices to be made by participants.

Responding to Participants' Emotional Preferences

The elements of motivation, persistence, responsibility, and structure can also be addressed by staff developers as they train participants in the use of technology.

Highly motivated participants will respond to interesting, cutting-edge topics that can be mastered in reasonable amounts of time. For less motivated participants, choose technology projects that are relevant, save time, and are practical for classroom use. There is little that is more motivating to teachers than to be helped to find a shortcut, and they want to be shown how to use database programs to record information concerning student growth and achievement. They also will appreciate learning how to use technology to communicate with parents easily (Vockell & Mihail, 1993).

To adapt instruction to varying persistence levels, trainers can offer work sessions where participants can complete one project from start to finish. On the other hand, global participants may need to work simultaneously on two or more projects, so be prepared with some of "the next session's work."

Responsibility, as an element of learning style, deals with whether a participant does as directed by the trainer or requires choices. Staff developers need to provide options with only limited input for some, and specific guidelines for others. By providing opportunities to both follow explicit instructions and to design and establish individual guidelines, staff developers will be responding to the participants' preferences for structure. Some need it; some do not.

Responding to Participants' Sociological Preferences

When individuals' sociological preferences for working alone, in a pair, in groups, with a facilitator, or in a varied setting are capitalized on by treatments that are congruent with their learning style, they become capable of significantly higher achievement (Dunn & Dunn, 1993). Certain technologies lend themselves well to cooperative learning activities, including those that use computer-based simulations and computer conferencing (Norris, 1994). And, with little effort, staff developers can meet the preferences of those individuals who prefer to work alone or in pairs.

Responding to Participants' Physiological Preferences

The physiological elements of the Dunn and Dunn Learning Styles Model include perceptual preferences (auditory, visual, kinesthetic, and tactual), intake, time, and mobility. Multimedia presentations, scanning, and the use of digital cameras appeal to visual learners. Auditory learners respond to lectures, recordings, and telecommunications. Tactual learners thrive on note-taking guides and keyboarding and also enjoy touch screens and graphic tablets, whereas interactive software is a vital component for kinesthetic learners.

Because some teachers prefer to attend workshops during the school day and others prefer late afternoons or summers, offering choices can facilitate meeting these time preferences and relieve participants' stress. McLean's "triune brain theory" explains why teachers who are anxious or concerned about being away from their classes may be inhibited from gaining as much as they can from staff development (Raupers, 1996). Staff developers who provide (1) modest snacks, (2) in-service before, during, or after school and in the summer months, (3) frequent breaks, and (4) opportunities for mobility during practice sessions are accommodating three learning-style traits—intake, time, and mobility preferences.

Responding to Participants' Processing Styles

For the analytic and left-hemisphere-dominant Helens in the workshop, staff developers need to provide solid reasons for using technology, combined with step-by-step instruction with detailed reference notes. Such persons also find it helpful to have sequential tasks. However, for the global, right-hemisphere-dominant Marys, staff developers need to provide anecdotal overviews replete with illustrations and some humor, minimal direct instruction, and opportunities for exploration. Graphic organizers and representations provide an important component for these participants.

Reflective learners require quiet time to review and absorb directions and information prior to application activities. Impulsive learners are happy when given the option to jump in and learn by discovery and experimentation (Dunn & Dunn, 1993).

When staff developers are sensitive to learning-style preferences, they can maximize training experiences. Participants are then able to focus their attention on the advantages and types of technology available to them. Instruction requires complex decision making. Teachers will be better able to make appropriate and effective technological choices for classroom use when staff development experiences are positive and meaningful to them. Giving teachers increased autonomy in curricular, instructional, and assessment decisions, and supporting them with professional development that is responsive to their learning styles, gradually empower them to create more effective schools (Darling-Hammond, 1996).

Subsequent Sessions

Follow-up training should include time with colleagues for activities centered about developing meaningful and practical applications of technology for their classes (Goldenberg & Gallimore, 1991). When staff developers apply aspects of the Dunn and Dunn model to their teacher in-service sessions, they model what is frequently asked of teachers: sensitivity to how diverse students learn—their learning styles.

HELEN AND MARY REVISITED

When the staff development team began working with Helen and Mary, they recognized the importance of providing instruction that matched both Helen's and Mary's learning-style preferences. They then developed a short individual plan for each teacher.

Helen, who was analytic, needed training that provided logical, sequential directions; a brightly lit, quiet environment that included conventional seating;

opportunities to work alone or with one of the staff developers; verbal and written instructions; step-by-step lessons where details and facts built on each other logically; and well-structured assignments that required some creative applications of the technology that had been introduced in that session.

Mary, who was global, needed training that provided anecdotal, amusing overviews that related the content directly to her classes' needs; an environment that allowed for sound, soft lighting, and informal seating; peer interactions and support from colleagues; visual and kinesthetic demonstrations; images and pictures for meaning; and opportunities to learn by exploring and discovering.

After receiving training that matched their individual learning-style preferences, Mary and Helen were able to apply what they had learned about technology to their classroom instruction. Mary, in particular, felt newly confident and gradually introduced the instructional strategies that made the most sense to her. In time, she modified what she had been shown and taught herself skills beyond those she had learned during the technology staff development.

Helen was exhilarated by her training experiences. Her intuitive feel for the use of technology had been validated and she had gained many new insights and skills. She quickly began incorporating what she had learned into her instructional repertoire and made many personal adaptations for her students. The staff development team was pleased that both teachers moved beyond the initial level of merely applying what they had learned. Helen looked forward to more training in the latest technologies available. Mary, on the other hand, was content to use what she had mastered. However, she no longer feared the use of technology and she recognized that her "toolbox" of teaching strategies had been expanded by the insights and skills gained during her recent professional development. At times, it almost seemed as if she had actually befriended her mouse!

REFERENCES

Association for Supervision and Curriculum Development. (1992). *Teaching to learning styles*. Alexandria, VA: Author.

Darling-Hammond, L. (1996). The quiet revolution: Rethinking teacher development. *Educational Leadership, 53*(6), 4–10.

Dunn, R., & Dunn, K. (1993). *Teaching secondary students through their individual learning styles*. Boston: Allyn & Bacon.

Dunn, R., Griggs, S., Olson, J., Beasley, M., & Gorman, B. (1995). A meta-analytic validation of the Dunn and Dunn model of learning style preferences. *Journal of Educational Research, 88*(6), 353–362.

Goldenberg, C., & Gallimore, R. (1991). Changing teaching takes more than a one-shot workshop. *Educational Leadership, 49*(3), 69–72.

Griggs, D., Griggs, S., Dunn, R., & Ingham, J. (1994). Accommodating nursing students' diverse learning styles. *Nurse Educator, 19*(6), 41–45.

Ingham, J. (1991). Matching instruction with employee perceptual preferences significantly increases training effectiveness. *Human Resource Development Quarterly, 2*(1), 53–64.

Norris, C. (1994, February). Computing and the classroom: Teaching the at-risk student. *The Computing Teacher*, 12–14.

Peck, K., & Dorricott, D. (1994). Why use technology? *Educational Leadership, 51*(7), 11–14.

Raupers, P. (1996). A learning-styles approach to staff development. *Focus on Education, 40,* 38–40.

Vockell, E., & Mihail, T. (1993, Spring). Principles behind computerized instruction for students with exceptionalities. *Teaching Exceptional Children,* 39–43.

6

Responding to Participants' Learning Styles: Hear, See, Touch, and Move Them!

Karen Burke

An attractive flyer appeared in the faculty room announcing an exciting workshop on "The Thrill of Teaching." The workshop would be held from 12:00 P.M. to 2:00 P.M. on the upcoming professional day. Mrs. Samide hadn't signed up for any required workshop. "Oh well," she thought as she gulped down her lunch, "this looks okay. I'll register for this one and get it over with."

On the day of the workshop, she attended meetings at school in the morning and rushed to be at the local university for the noon meeting. She had no time to stop for lunch because she wasn't sure where the meeting would be held. As she hurried through the parking lot, a thought occurred to her: "Now what was the title of that session?"

The lecture was to be held in Andrew Auditorium. Three hundred participants had signed up. Mrs. Samide slipped into the back row and quickly pulled out yesterday's math tests to mark. "If I only had a cup of coffee and a place to put my feet up, this would be a perfect workshop!" Apparently the teacher sitting next to her felt the same way. She had already read the New York Times *and was now knitting a lovely sweater. Upon leaving the auditorium, Mrs. Samide overheard a comment: "Why do we have to put up with this staff development nonsense?" "I don't understand her problem," she thought. "This workshop was fine and I even completed my plan book for next week!"*

This depiction of an in-service day is typical of what occurs in too many school systems. That may be why staff development has been referred to as neglected and ineffective by Wood and Thompson (1980). Yet we also have been told that the future of the school climate will be largely dependent on how staff development evolves (Joyce, 1993).

Why are we dealing with a dichotomous situation? Staff development has attracted a great deal of attention in recent years. Until 1957, only about 50 studies had been completed on staff development (Showers, Joyce, & Bennett, 1987). Now, more than three times that number of studies are being conducted every year. Considerable research exists on in-service programs: Berman and McLaughlin (1978), Lawrence (1974), Mohlman, Kierstead, and Gundlach (1982), and Showers, Joyce, and Bennett (1987). The research is there, but many educators have continued to plan and implement in-service education based on faulty assumptions of some research or no research at all. If staff developers are to plan and implement effective programs that improve teaching and learning, it is important that their actions be guided by a set of assumptions that are grounded in research and best practice (Wood & Thompson, 1993).

Perhaps the most vital development in American education today is the concept of individual learners' preferences (DeBello, 1990). Extensive, well-conducted research verifies the existence of individual differences among all learners—yes, even teachers. If staff development is to be effective, we need to identify the learning styles of all participants and then use practical approaches for presenting in-service through their unique learning-style strengths.

Learning style encompasses at least 20 variables, including each person's environmental, emotional, sociological, physiological, and cognitive-processing preferences. It is important to identify learning style with a comprehensive instrument, and it is critical to use one that is both reliable and valid (Dunn & Dunn, 1992).

The Productivity Environmental Preference Survey (PEPS) (Dunn, Dunn, & Price, 1982) is a measurement of the learning-style preferences of adults. The measure consists of 100 dichotomous questions that elicit self-diagnostic responses relating to 20 discrete learning-style elements. The PEPS is a comprehensive approach to the identification of how adults prefer to function, learn, concentrate, and perform in their occupational or educational activities. Careful analysis of each person's PEPS profile will identify those elements that are essential to an individual's success in learning new and difficult material.

Just as it is important for teachers to plan instruction based upon what they know about how students learn, so staff developers need to be much more aware of how adults learn and the implications of this for designing and implementing in-service programs. Knowledge about adult learners should serve as the basis for planning and implementation of staff development (Wood & Thompson, 1993).

ENVIRONMENTALLY SPEAKING

Does This Sound Familiar? Have You Ever Felt This Way?

- "Is this building air conditioned, or are we going to fry this afternoon?"
- "Just tell me, who invented the metal folding chair? It's not for humans!"
- "The lights in this room make me feel as if I'm in the spotlight."

- "Do you think they paid their electric bill?"
- "I wish the people around me would keep quiet so I can concentrate."

How Can Staff Developers Respond to the Environmental Elements?

Few people are aware that, when a person is seated in a hard chair, approximately 75 percent of his or her total body weight is resting on four square inches of bone (Branton, 1966). No wonder teachers cannot wait for a session to end so they can get up and move around.

In-service sessions cannot be conducted in the same environment for all teachers at the same time (Dunn, Dunn, & Freeley, 1985). Some teachers may need soft music playing while others remain in a totally quiet area. Some will prefer well-illuminated rooms while others will absorb the new material only when the lights are low.

Five Ways to Respond Environmentally

1. Check whether the room will maintain a comfortable temperature. A room that feels comfortable when only a few people are present can become oppressively hot when full to capacity. Provide fans, open windows, heaters, and so forth in different parts of the room.

2. Teachers will react more positively in a comfortable atmosphere. Wherever possible provide tables, padded chairs, couches, ottomans, and so on.

3. Make sure the facility is appropriate for the activity. For example, small-group discussions held in an auditorium with fixed seating can give teachers stiff necks and a negative attitude toward future in-service sessions.

4. Provide both bright and low-light areas.

5. See that all equipment is operating correctly so that all the participants can hear and see what is presented. Check the microphones, cassettes, and overheads. Don't forget to check the plugs and outlets as well. Remember that many a disaster can be avoided if you bring along extra bulbs and extension cords.

EMOTIONALLY SPEAKING

Does This Sound Familiar? Have You Ever Felt This Way?

- "I've been teaching for 20 years. Why do I have to go to this workshop?"
- "Two hours and no break! I usually stop every half-hour when I'm working."
- "How many workshops must I go to this year?"
- "My teaching contract indicates that I have to attend four in-service sessions this year? I'd rather visit other schools and learn about new programs by observing them in action."

How Can Staff Developers Respond to the Emotional Elements?

Most adults want to be involved directly in their own learning. They often become defensive when administrators or presenters are perceived to be downgrading their teaching competence. Instructors should aid in setting goals, priorities, and the processes of staff development.

Because participants have a wide range of previous experiences, knowledge, interests, competencies, and motivation, they will learn, retain, and use what they perceive is relevant to their personal and professional needs. Staff development must enable teachers and administrators to see the relationship between what they are learning and their day-to-day activities and problems (Wood & Thompson, 1993).

Five Ways to Respond Emotionally

1. Encourage teachers to design and participate in the presentation of strategies and materials. This approach is likely to improve their attitudes toward in-service.

2. Schedule social time at the beginning of each session. Serving refreshments encourages a relaxed start and promotes a relaxed transition to work.

3. When beginning, review the structure of the session for the participants. Inform them when breaks will be scheduled.

4. Utilize icebreakers that build group rapport, introduce participants to each other, and establish a nurturing atmosphere.

5. Provide question time for those participants who may desire more structure, direction, or feedback than others. Request feedback after the session by providing evaluation forms.

SOCIOLOGICALLY SPEAKING

Does This Sound Familiar? Have You Ever Felt This Way?

- "I just wish I could talk to the other teachers to see how they feel."
- "Are we going to have to do any of that 'sharing and caring' in groups?"
- "I'm tired of hearing her talk. I'd prefer to listen to a variety of people."
- "That teacher thinks she knows it all. I hope I don't wind up in her group."

How Can Staff Developers Respond to the Sociological Elements?

Lecturing has long been the established method of providing staff development. Unfortunately, this expedient method undoubtedly continues, but it should be modified with other techniques and eventually discarded, except for auditory, listen-alone learners. Many adults will respond best to a learning situation that groups them with one to four of their peers. They may need the interaction with their colleagues both to stimulate them to learn and to provide motivation. For this reason, many participants' learning styles are best served if they are permitted to work in small groups during workshops. Groups provide structure and varied interactions as well. Options should be available for those who prefer to work alone.

Some adults need variety and should have options and chances in presenting to alleviate boredom. Other participants may very well prefer the security of repeated instructional routines and procedural patterns.

Five Ways to Respond Sociologically

1. Minimize talking at the staff and maximize staff interaction and activities.
2. Include small-group discussions where teachers and administrators have an opportunity to share, reflect, and generalize from their experiences.
3. Do not require all participants to move into small groups to perform the required tasks; offer options for those who prefer to work alone or with only one partner.
4. Provide short lectures with varied learning activities to follow.
5. Encourage an exchange of ideas to promote a collegial atmosphere. A good facilitator doesn't permit one person or group to monopolize the time. Participants acting as reporters or recorders of information contribute to the development of the learning.

PHYSIOLOGICALLY SPEAKING

Does This Sound Familiar? Have You Ever Felt This Way?

- "Where's the coffee?"
- "Do you think our district has stock in Dunkin Donuts? That's all we ever get here."
- "This is my nap time; I can't keep my eyes open."
- "How much longer will I have to sit here with my legs crossed before he gives us a break?"
- "Just give me the handouts and stop talking about it."

How Can Staff Developers Respond to the Physiological Elements?

Viewing the teacher as a whole person with many and varied physiological needs must be widely embraced by staff developers. These needs include hunger, time-of-day preferences, mobility requirements, and perceptual preferences. In the business world employers would rarely ask employees to be at their best for learning new ideas after 4:00 P.M. on a busy day, with the only lure being a meager cup of coffee.

Time-of-day as well as intake preferences should be considered by those planning staff development.

When adults were introduced to new material through their perceptual preferences, they remembered significantly more than when they were taught through other modalities (Ingham, 1991). It is necessary, therefore, that staff developers should design auditory, visual, tactual, and kinesthetic materials and match them with each learner's strength.

Five Ways to Respond Physiologically

1. Provide a variety of snacks and drinks for participants throughout the entire workshop.

2. Wherever possible, schedule teachers at the time of day that corresponds to their highest energy levels.

3. Videotape presentations for use by teachers at whichever time of day they prefer.

4. Provide opportunities as well as freedom to move around during the session.

5. Vary the instructional resources to present the material through different perceptual strengths. Tactual/kinesthetic materials should be available for those participants who prefer them.

SUMMARY

Matching strategies for staff development with learning-style strengths is important to successful in-service just as the same positive approach in the classroom is. Research reveals in study after study that adults who learn in a program that accommodates their preferences achieve increased knowledge, become more motivated, and utilize what they learn in the classroom. If we design staff development programs in this fashion, Mrs. Samide might mark her tests and do her plan book at a time other than during the in-service workshop!

REFERENCES

Berman, P., & McLaughlin, M. W. (1978). *Federal programs supporting educational change, Vol. 8: Implementing and sustaining innovations* (ED 159 289). Santa Monica, CA: Rand Corp.

Branton, P. (1966). *The comfort of easy chairs* (FIRA Technical Report 22). Hertfordshire, England: Furniture Industry Research Association.

DeBello, T. (1990). Comparison of eleven major learning style models: Variables, appropriate populations, validity of instrumentation, and the research behind them. *Journal of Reading, Writing, and Learning Disabilities International, 6*(3), 315–322.

Diegmueller, K. (1991). Nourishing hearts, minds, and bodies. *Journal of Staff Development, 12*(4), 6–8.

Dunn, K., Dunn, R., & Freeley, M. E. (1985). Tips to improve your inservice training. *Early Years, 4,* 30–31.

Dunn, K., Dunn, R., & Price, G. E. (1982). *Productivity Environmental Preference Survey.* Obtainable from Price Systems, Box 1818, Lawrence, KS, 66044.

Dunn, R., & Dunn, K. (1992). *Teaching elementary students through their individual learning styles.* Boston, MA: Allyn & Bacon.

Ingham, J. (1991). Matching instruction with employee perceptual preferences significantly increases training effectiveness. *Human Resource Development Quarterly, 2*(1), 53–64.

Ingham, J., & Dunn, R. (1993). The Dunn and Dunn model of learning styles: Addressing learning diversity. *The 1993 Annual Developing Human Resources.* London: Pieffer and Co.

Joyce, B. (1993). Four responses to Orlich and others. *Journal of Staff Development, 14*(3), 10–17.

Joyce, B. R., & Showers, B. (1980). Improving inservice training: The message of research. *Educational Leadership, 37,* 379–385.

Lawrence, G. (1974). Patterns of effective in-service education: A state of the art summary of research on materials and procedures for changing teacher behaviors in in-service education (ED 176 424). Tallahassee, FL: Florida State Department of Education.

Mohlman, G. G., Kierstead, J., & Gundlach, M. (1982). A research-based in-service model for secondary teachers. *Educational Leadership, 40*(1), 16–19.

Showers, B., Joyce, B., & Bennett, B. (1987). Synthesis of research on staff development: A framework for future study and a state of the analysis. *Educational Leadership, 45*(7), 77–87

Wood, F. W., & Thompson, S. R. (1980). Guidelines for better staff development. *Educational Leadership, 37*(5), 374–378.

Wood, F. W., & Thompson, S. R. (1993). Assumptions about staff development based on research and best practice. *Journal of Staff Development, 14*(4), 52–56.

7

A Closer Look at Selection: Staff Development Instructors or Destructors?

Deborah O'Connell-Brebbia

> *Mary:* "Hi, Regina, how's it going?"
>
> *Regina:* "Everything is great! Tomorrow we don't have school, so I'm watching TV tonight."
>
> *Mary:* "How come you don't have school?"
>
> *Regina:* "I don't know—some superintendent's conference day."
>
> *Mary:* "What's that?"
>
> *Regina:* "It's when the teachers learn something new, try it out on us the next day, and things are back to normal the day after."
>
> *Mary:* "Wow, that sounds exciting!"
>
> *Regina:* "Yeah, I can't wait for the next superintendent's conference day!"

Staff development programs have earned a tarnished reputation because of "one-shot" professional presentations. Educators are skeptical when they have to attend one-day sessions and often resist because they feel it is a waste of time. How did this happen? In the past, what teachers needed to know was crammed into a day or two, often delivered by a visiting guru who blew into town briefly and was never seen again (Lewis, 1994). How did the idea of increasing professionals' abilities turn into a charade? With this question in mind, it is crucial for educators to examine in-service programs in depth, with most of the effort focused on the selection of the instructors and consultants. No longer should an expert be hired just because he or she does not live within 50 miles or because he or she happens to be a friend of the superintendent. This chapter will focus on the criteria for selecting and the evaluation process which should be established in order to select the quality staff developers that match a school's or district's needs.

DO WE REALLY NEED THIS?

The first step when choosing a program is to assess the faculty's need for that training. There is little chance for implementation of a program if the faculty isn't interested or sees no personal or staff gain. Using a short assessment survey, administrators can gain a greater insight into the position of the faculty on many issues. The first responsibility of any staff developer or committee is to conduct a thorough needs assessment, including teachers' needs, school's needs, district's needs, and students' needs (Purvis & Brown, 1991). Why bring an innovation to the faculty if time can be spent in a more meaningful way? A needs assessment would be a tremendous motivator because teachers would feel that their opinions count. Gone should be the days when teachers await a memo to inform them of the agenda for the superintendent's conference day. It is important that each school have a clear vision, and a shared vision is a powerful force toward shaping staff attitudes and behavior (Sparks, 1992). Once a need is established, the work should begin to find the perfect person or team for the task. This will not be an easy task, but it is the most crucial step in the entire process. If an administrator loses credibility during this initial stage, there is no hope for future staff development training to be successful.

Administrators should also consider the time of day the program is to be offered. Studies have demonstrated that when teachers were taught during their time-of-day preference for the training, they actually implemented the instructional technique in the classroom (Dunn, Dunn, & Freeley, 1985). In addition to providing staff development at alternative times during the day, developers can provide many forms of training (Sparks, 1992).

THE SELECTION PROCESS—"EENY, MEENY, MINY, MO"

The process of selecting a staff developer is a grueling one, and educators should be prepared to devote time and effort to the task. Once the program goals are determined, a representative or team should decide who will be the most effective leader or leaders of the program (Purvis, 1991). The team should investigate the experience and expertise of the intended staff developer. Most developers "take their act on the road," so the first step in the process of selection should be to observe the person(s) in action. This step is similar to hearing a musical band for your wedding. Engaged couples travel from nightclub to nightclub to listen to bands. They enjoy good food and share future dreams while listening to the band play. Similarly, the selection team needs to see the developer in action. Is the developer actively engaging the group? Are the participants interested or are they talking or reading newspapers in the rear? Are these participants similar to yours? How well does the presenter field questions? How confident is the presenter? Do you want to hear more from that presenter?

Viewing the presenter at work is much better than getting secondhand testimonials, and the team will have a better feeling about whether or not to hire him or her. In many cases, viewing the consultant in action might be impossible, because of time or travel constraints. If this is the case, the representative can elicit feedback from previous engagements and view videotapes of the expert's repertoire. This will not be as effective as viewing the presenter in person, but it is better than not having any prior knowledge before he or he steps foot into your school.

The second step in the selection process is to review the staff developer's resume very carefully. This is a perfect opportunity to inquire about the research supporting the in-service program and a chance to ask for the names and number of school districts implementing the program. Perhaps the developer has written published articles on the topic.

Thus far, the team can evaluate the following:

- the developer in action
- the developer's resume and credentials
- the current schools implementing the program
- the research on which the program is based
- published articles written by the developer
- success of the staff in using what they learned, for example, improved student scores, student self-image, and discipline

There really is no reason to look any further if the above results are disappointing. This particular presenter, then, would not be the person for your faculty.

However, if the consultant meets your needs, it is time to proceed to the next step in the process. At this point the team should assess the school's ability to afford the selected in-service program. What will the school get for its money? Does this price include follow-up visits? Does this price include the option to contact the developer when the program is put into action? Personal contact is crucial when implementing a new program. Can faculty members contact the developer via e-mail, the telephone, or by other means of communication? Will there be a considerable amount of follow-through when the school begins implementation? This is one way to find out if the consultant stands by his or her program.

This research has resulted in a great deal of knowledge about the staff developer under consideration. Gradually, the team has learned about the proposed staff development program. This will prove invaluable when the implementation phase begins. Now there will be many people within the district knowledgeable about the developer and the goals of the program.

THE CONTRACT—"SIGN ON THE DOTTED LINE"

Now that the preliminary work has been completed, it is time to draw up a contract. The team and developer will be formalizing an agreement. Here the team should address all their concerns and specifically state every detail of their needs.

All particulars of the deal should be ironed out and placed in writing, and perhaps a statement of consequence should be added specifying what will happen if the developer does not fulfill the requirements of the contract. Indeed, a performance contract including basic fees, rewards, and deductions is rarely consummated but should be considered.

LARGE-SCALE REFORM

Many staff development programs prepare school districts for large-scale reform. For teachers to use a new technique effectively, they must possess a knowledge of the technique, a positive attitude toward it, and the necessary skills to implement it successfully in class (Melnick, 1991). If the staff developer has been selected carefully, teachers will be better able to implement large-scale reform.

The day finally arrives, and the presenter is all set up and ready to roll. The faculty are greeted and the program begins. Since a lot of preliminary work has been completed, the team has a good idea of what to expect from the day. Team members should be randomly placed in the room and should actively participate in the formal training. As the day continues, the team should, if possible, identify additional faculty members who show enthusiasm for the program. These faculty members may be asked to receive additional training to implement the program effectively.

A grave mistake many districts make is to create the feeling that staff development is an isolated event. Instead of remaining with a particular program until it has been mastered, these districts set up another new program hot on the previous one's tail. No sooner do teachers file their notes away from one new approach than they are required to collect a new set. Since teachers are the pivotal players in the reform movement, it is crucial to remain with a program until teachers reach a level of comfort and expertise.

THE ROAD LONELY TRAVELED

Wow! The developer gave us a great binder for all our notes, team activities, and many reproducibles. How should I use all this in my classroom? Well, let me start small and build from there. Here we go! Did he say to introduce topic A and then try activity A, or was I to do KWL, or cooperative groups, or . . .

The scenario written here is not an uncommon one experienced by teachers. Many honestly try to implement a new program in their classrooms, but when the presenter has gone, teachers often find that "doing it" is an overwhelming task. The teacher is back in the classroom, alone and with nowhere to turn. Some teachers find it difficult to reach out and ask for help. The teacher is, once again, traveling the road alone. Worse, staff development programs commonly lack follow-through. This happens to be one of the greatest criticisms of such programs. To avoid adding one more new thing to the pile, the team must be ready for action. This can be referred to as the maintenance phase of program development. It is a critical step in the process. All too often teachers attend staff development programs and learn new techniques, but do not take what they have learned and use it on the job (Purvis, 1991).

DON'T MAKE A MOUNTAIN OUT OF A MOLEHILL

A few days after the initial exposure to the program, it is quite possible that the faculty begins to feel frustrated. Everything seemed so easy when the presenter was around, but now they don't know what to do. Here the team must rekindle the fire without a time gap. The team needs to provide some ongoing training. This would probably be an appropriate time to gather the faculty members together again. The team could thank their colleagues for their effort and then slowly review the important points of the program. Preferably using a small-group activity, the faculty members could reinforce the newly learned material.

"DON'T CRY OVER SPILT COFFEE"

It is possible that, despite earnest efforts, the program may still not be working. Perhaps a lesson or two did not reap the rewards teachers thought it would. Most programs will take time to get off the ground. Immediately, the team should contact the presenter. Remember, the team made it clear in the contractual agreement that there would be a considerable amount of follow-through; perhaps an additional meeting with the team is needed. The team should assess the progress of the program implementation to this point. Trying to elicit honest responses from the faculty would be a great place to start. The team can look over the results of the assessment and see if it is time to call upon the presenter.

"YOU CAN LEAD A DONKEY TO WATER, BUT YOU CAN'T MAKE IT DRINK"

Even with the most successful programs, we can expect some teachers to offer resistance. Administrators expect to hear a litany of common sayings:

- Our problem is different.
- We tried that once before.
- Been there; done that.
- We've always done it this way.
- You can't teach an old dog new tricks.
- Let's make a report/form a committee.
- It can't work with these children.
- I'm overworked now.
- What? *Another* new fad?
- My administrator will not let me do *that!*

The list can go on and on. All programs will not be accepted as quickly as one could hope. This should not discourage the team, which has a responsibility to the district and to the faculty members who are interested. Good programs have a way of becoming woven into the fabric of a district. With a lot of hard work, a dedicated and professional team, and perseverance, the program can be implemented.

THE DOMINO EFFECT

A quick review of the process brings our focus back to the presenter. The presenter sparked interest among the team members; the team excited the faculty. The presenter meets with the faculty; the team works with the faculty; the faculty inspires the children. Here we clearly see the effects of a staff development program when it is researched correctly. Somehow along the way, these programs too often are not connected with professional development and student achievement. Professional development is an integral part of the change/reform effort. Educating and training programs must be selected carefully so that their impact is far-reaching. A vital part of reform is the acceptance of the program by the faculty. This acceptance will create a positive climate for reform efforts.

TIME TO CELEBRATE A JOB WELL DONE

After all the planning and implementation of staff development, it's time to sit back and see how the program is running. It is also time to begin to evaluate the program. Participants in the program should have the chance to evaluate the presentation and the program itself and be offered the opportunity to discuss their perceptions with colleagues. A formal questionnaire is helpful to assess both. This questionnaire will guide the team to further improve future staff development programs. Having time to discuss the presentation may clear up any questions the participants may have and afford the opportunity to discuss the questions with the presenter before his or her departure.

As we are constantly assessing student outcomes, we should assess whether or not this in-service addressed the school's needs. When the team keeps the school's needs in mind and makes decisions based on what is best for children, success is likely to follow. Obviously, it is critical to measure each staff development's impact on meeting a school's success as projected in its mission and yearly goals.

REFERENCES

Dunn, K., Dunn, R., & Freeley, M. (1985). Tips to improve your inservice training. *Early Years, 15*(8), 30–31.

Lewis, A. (1994). Developing good staff development. *Phi Delta Kappan, 75*(7), 508–509.

Melnick, S. (1991). High school staff development: Matching activities to outcomes. *NASSP Bulletin, 75*(536), 60–64.

Purvis, J., & Brown, L. (1991). Planning and implementing a staff development program. *NASSP Bulletin, 75*(536), 16–23.

Sparks, D. (1992). The keys to effective staff development. *Principal, 71*(3), 43–44.

8

Evaluation of Professional Development: Do the Bosses Make the Grade?

Eric Brand and Susan Brand

Professional development often strikes fear in the hearts of anyone who has taught for more than a few hours. With a world full of so many charming and intellectual people, we must wonder why it is that so few of them become professional development providers. People's evaluations of professional development could form a simple top 10 list à la David Letterman:

10. At least there is money in it.
9. I get to actually see my colleagues.
8. You get stuff.
7. They are held in fun places.
6. We get to watch our bosses teach.
5. Here we go again.
4. I love the stale coffee and day-old Danish.
3. I get to see what others are doing.
2. It gives me another reason to stay after school.

And the number one evaluation of professional development is: I hope I die at a professional development session because the transition will be easier.

These attitudes pose a dilemma for those trying to improve staff development. Most people agree that professional development is important. Regardless of one's starting point, research has shown that first-year teachers' successes are dependent on the schools in which they teach. They will get better—or not—depending on the professional development they receive. The continued development of teaching staff is important in bringing new ideas to the classroom as well as in defeating the ominous beast of burnout. One problem with present professional development is incomplete evaluation. Because evaluation is not meaningful, programs do not improve. Lack of evaluation contributes to the cycle of poor professional development, which, in turn, leads to teachers' negative attitudes.

We often hear that professional development is key to instructional improvement. But how do we evaluate and change these programs to defeat the attitude that professional development is just a matter of hiring another expert with new buzzwords for the same thing? Little has promised so much but has been so shamefully wasteful as the thousands of workshops and conferences that have led to no significant change or new meaning for the educators. Few on either side of the professional development classroom are happy about the results of professional development programs. Here are the top 10 reasons most professional development fails:

10. Topics selected by someone other than the teachers
 9. Mostly nonexistent follow-up support
 8. The widespread use of one-shot workshops to solve problems
 7. Programs that rarely meet individual needs of participants
 6. No recognition that each school in a district may be unique
 5. Not enough time allocated to plan and learn new skills and practices
 4. Tendencies to try quick-fix solutions
 3. Underfunding of new ideas
 2. Lack of cohesion or sustained support and follow-through from the central office

And the *number one reason* professional development fails is: Evaluation, if it occurs at all, occurs only on the day of the workshop and is never used to improve the program.

This list may make it seem that the beast of burnout will never be defeated. One of the reasons professional development fails is that insufficient time is allocated to the evaluation process. "What about all those evaluation forms we fill out?" you may ask. Evaluation must go beyond completion of a questionnaire at the end of a session. Evaluation must begin before the session and continue into the classroom.

Evaluating staff development correctly is extremely time-consuming because of the complexity of analyzing the data generated. If, as the Rolling Stones sang, "Time is on my side, yes it is," then it is clear that Mick Jagger is not, nor ever was, an educator! Teachers need time to evaluate their professional development needs, to critically evaluate the in-service they have received, and, later, to try out the new methods. Time is then needed for teachers to meet with colleagues to evaluate what's working and what's not working in their classrooms to determine whether problems are unique to them or endemic. Sufficient time must be given for teachers to iron out and retry techniques. Professional developers need time to process evaluations, in order to identify successful activities and presenters for later use, to provide feedback to teachers based on the assessments, and to adjust training to incorporate feedback. They also need time for classroom visitations to observe the new techniques in action and for follow-up meetings and seminars with teachers. Time must be given to make the critical adjustments to ensure that participants master and use the techniques as intended. A great deal of time is essential for even true evaluation to change the attitudes of teachers attending professional development.

For evaluation to improve the intellectual development of teachers, professional development providers cannot continue to instruct teachers on better methodology without questioning their own methodology. Professional development providers must ask themselves and teachers, "What do you need to know and how can we help you learn it?" This questioning is the initial step toward improved evaluation of professional development. The genesis of evaluation should not be at 3:00 on the day of the workshop but at the initial stages of planning. Evaluation should then continue throughout the implementation and follow-up phases. Just as professional development providers are responsible for evaluation to make programs better, all educators share responsibility for evaluation and modification. As part of the evaluative planning process, staff developers should consider teacher motivation. To motivate the school community, recognize that, to improve, we need to forgo the notion that teaching is merely altruistic. Teachers cannot foster students' intellectual development if their own is not fostered. Furthermore, educators need to foster the intellectual development of all members of their community. When seeking to increase teacher motivation, professional development providers need also to consider teachers' learning and teaching styles.

Teacher education—preservice, in-service, and graduate programs—is a seemingly endless continuum of professional development. However, teachers' attitudes seem to be one of derision for each of these stages. Districts try to keep their staff's minds sharp with a plethora of professional opportunities, but districts often fall short because of poor evaluation of staff needs and ineffective programs.

As part of the planning process, teachers should be provided with well-presented, well-researched methods and then be encouraged to evaluate them. Again, their evaluations should be analyzed on the basis of their learning styles, for different people perceive the same approaches differently.

Professional development is multifaceted and continuous. From the moment a person decides to become a teacher to the moment he or she attends the first education course, that person is excited about taking courses toward his or her new profession. Gradually, wonderment disappears and the arduous search for relevance from the college classroom to the one he or she will occupy commences. Undergraduate work, methods of teaching, practice teaching, and actual teaching have been like islands in a large lake; you can see that they have similar vegetation from the shore but there is no way to get from one to the other without a boat. Professional development programs lack the coherence that bridges provide: Evaluation and the subsequent adjustment of programs are one way of building the bridges. Another is involving teachers in a number of purposeful teaching settings to acquire and hone the skills and habits of working with a variety of situations and strategies. Clinical supervision—with its emphasis on improving, rather than evaluating, a teacher's skills in a collegial manner—is another.

Once these commitments and procedures are designed and professional development has begun, thorough evaluation of the staff development sessions should be conducted. This can be time-consuming, if done well, and it requires a responsibility to put the data collected to good use. Evaluation should ensure that staff reaction and perceptions are accurate; adjustments are made as needed; successful activities are identified; outstanding presenters are brought back; success or failure of a project can be determined early; long- and short-range profiles are compiled; and most important for the continuation of effective evaluation, participants learn that their evaluations matter.

The evaluation of professional development implementation should be a two-to-three-step process. The first evaluation about the nature of the workshop should be done immediately on site. This evaluation would examine first impressions—such as the effectiveness of the instructor and the session, whether the session met the needs of the participants, and most important, what teachers might actually use from the session. This formative evaluation would provide immediate feedback so that problems can be quickly identified and resolved and the program as a whole would be improved.

The second evaluation, given a short time later, should ask whether or not the first impression remains the same. The evaluation should ask what was gained, what techniques the teacher has tried or is planning to try, and what concerns the teacher has about the method(s). Concerns should then be addressed by the staff developer. To get a true response, it is imperative that evaluation be nonthreatening and collegial.

The third phase of evaluation, approximately four weeks later, should address previously mentioned concerns and solicit reactions to how those concerns are being addressed. This step in the process would ask which techniques have been tried, what has been successful, and what has not. Again, an atmosphere of collegiality needs to be fostered to ensure that teachers feel free to admit problems and share concerns. This collegiality makes the evaluation a two-way street; both sides are working together to make the program meaningful so that it increases the effectiveness of instruction.

To merely evaluate professional developers would be wasteful. We must also examine the teachers' role in their own learning. For professional development to be effective, teachers should make several commitments. First, teachers should become aware of a need to evaluate their own teaching style. Teachers who believe they need to be lifelong learners will model that belief for their students. This modeling will be a fringe benefit of the rewards the teachers will find when examining how they teach in comparison with how their students learn.

Second, teachers should make a written commitment to put into effect pertinent ideas from the professional development workshops. Often teachers, like most people, resort to the minimum level of energy. New methods often take more time and energy in the initial phases of implementation. Also, teachers need to commit to modifying the ideas they take from the workshop to meet their own classes' unique needs. To do this, teachers need to become more research oriented. They must try the new ideas and evaluate whether or not they have been more effective than previous methods. Teachers also should commit to observe other teachers' classrooms and analyze the successes and failures of their colleagues collegially.

Teachers need to be able to report failures as well as successes with new programs. Often we give lip service to a new method that someone else promotes, and yet we rarely implement it completely. For this reason, it is essential that fellow teachers and the professional development provider observe us implementing. Observations must be done in a collegial fashion to be successful.

Teachers need to be exposed to a variety of approaches implemented by master teachers; simulations, observations, critiques of videotapes, and presentations are also helpful. Goals should be set at easily attainable levels and also at higher, more aspiring ones. As goals are met, the teachers need to be encouraged. After all of these things are done, another evaluation must be introduced.

After a period of time in which teachers use some new methods, the educational leader should visit the class to observe implementation. Then, as part of the postobservation conference, the teacher and supervisor together should evaluate the program to date.

To combat the one-shot mentality of professional development, follow-up sessions or support must be provided in the teaching of any new technique. Follow-up sessions should be based on planning and implementation evaluations and should be evaluated themselves. These evaluations should investigate how the professional development follow-up contributed to the success or failure of the program. Interactive, thorough evaluations should occur throughout the planning, implementation, and follow-up phases in order to ensure that staff development programs are meaningful and result in improved instruction.

Final evaluations are used in a decision-making process in which it is decided whether to continue the project as is, modify and continue it, or terminate it. This summative evaluation would provide a profile of the whole program to determine its effectiveness. Group tests, student achievement tests, classroom observations, attitude scales, and anecdotal records should all be data to determine the effectiveness of staff development and the program the staff developers brought.

Once again it is time for a Top 10—this time a list of characteristics of successful teacher development:

10. Formal placement of the new program within the district's philosophy
9. Integration of individual goals with school or district goals
8. Design built on principles of adult learning
7. Appropriate incentives and rewards
6. Leadership and administrative support
5. Time to work on and assimilate new learning
4. Participant involvement in goal setting, implementing, evaluating, and decision making
3. Incorporation of available knowledge bases

2. Collegiality, collaboration, experimentation, and risk taking
1. Good evaluations!

PART II

USING LEARNING STYLES TO DEVELOP EFFECTIVE STAFF DEVELOPMENT PROGRAMS

9

Striking the Right Note: A Sound Way to Improve Staff Development

Jack Gremli

A young music teacher was out walking one night when six of his own students attacked him. They wanted an apology. The teacher had called one of them a "nanny-goat bassoonist"—someone who makes a bassoon sound like a goat. The teacher wouldn't take it back; he drew a knife in self-defense. Luckily the fight was broken up before anyone was really hurt.

That same teacher had trouble with people who didn't see things his way. He once wanted to quit a job, and his employer wanted him to stay. The teacher was so insistent on breaking the contract that his boss threw him into jail. But here is the difference between this music teacher and the average stubborn person: during the month he spent in jail, he wrote 46 pieces of music—music that we still listen to 300 years later (Krull, 1993, pp. 15–17).

That music teacher was Johann Sebastian Bach. Bach was challenged to write music every week and to grow as a choir director as well as a composer. Music was his vehicle and it certainly can play an important role in the process of learning. The purpose of this chapter is to suggest ways that music can be used in staff development and to suggest particular styles and composition titles (including some written by J. S. Bach himself) to use as a part of professional development.

The Bulgarian psychotherapist Georgi Lozanov (1978), through his system called Suggestopoedia, reported that traditional instruction tends to address only the cortical structures of the left hemisphere of the brain and ignores human beings' emotionality and subconscious involvement while involved in learning. Lozanov suggested strategies for stimulating people's (1) innate thirst for knowledge, (2) intuitive-creative tendencies, (3) global personality, and (4) use of subconscious foundation for activating long-term memory as the basis for developing Suggestopoedia. Lozanov believed that this system produces a pleasurable, natural learning process through the use of classical music, art, role-playing, and games.

Dunn and Waggoner (1995) reported that environmental sound, including music, is required by some people to concentrate, whereas others need absolute quiet when learning new and difficult material. Auditory preferences and the ability to concentrate in quiet, with background music, or in either condition have been factors in the study of individuals' learning styles (Dunn, 1987). Pizzo, Dunn, and Dunn (1990) reported that when environmental learning-style preferences were accommodated, achievement increased and attitude toward learning improved statistically.

Music can be a powerful tool when used during staff development. Playing music while the participants of the in-service workshop are entering the hall or room is an excellent way to create an appropriate ambiance for learning, sharing, and establishing a positive feeling about being there. Music should be selected to match the agenda of the session. For example, if the topic at hand is peer coaching, a selection of songs by the Beatles such as "With a Little Help from My Friends" or the theme from the television show *Friends*, "I'll Be There for You," might be appropriate. Handel's *Water Music* sets a mood of relaxed seriousness and would be ideal for thought-provoking, early-morning sessions.

A person's musical taste is as individual as his or her learning style. Staff developers should examine their audience, explore their own musical tastes, and choose music to play that the consultant finds appealing. Having that music in the air as the audience enters will introduce the presenter before anyone takes to the microphone. Music serves as a link among the participants in the workshop and focuses them on the work that lies ahead.

A unique and effective way of dividing into groups for breakout sessions is to have the participants seek others who share learning-style traits similar to theirs. People who prefer to concentrate with ambient sound should be encouraged to work together and should be guided to rooms or work areas where music is supplied for them. People who choose to concentrate alone *and* prefer background music can work in a separate section of the same working space. Thus, music will be present for all who desire it. Some may prefer quiet and they, too, should be accommodated (Gremli, 1996).

Music supplied for this purpose should not contain lyrics. It is to serve as an unobtrusive stimulus for learning. The presence of lyrics will distract the conscious thought process from the task at hand and focus it instead on interpretation of the lyrics. Ideal music for this purpose is any instrumental selection from the baroque period. This era's musical compositions tend to be more mathematical in structure and are not as emotionally charged as music from, for example, the romantic period. The extremes of dynamic levels are less in baroque music than in music from other eras; consequently, there is less chance that the element of aural surprise will distract a listener from the academic agenda. Antonio Vivaldi, George Frideric Handel, and Johann Sebastian Bach are excellent sources of music for this purpose. The compositions of W. A. Mozart that clearly display Bach's influence on Mozart are also appropriate. Researchers have found that exposure to Mozart's Sonata for Two Pianos in D Major, K. 448 results in considerably improved performance by students in intelligence tests (Rauscher, Shaw, & Ky, 1993).

Equally as effective is the cool jazz of Tom Scott or David Benoit. Bobby McFerrin produced compact discs and tapes that bridge the classical and jazz idioms. Table 9.1 presents a list of musical suggestions for use during staff development. "Easy listening" arrangements of popular tunes should be avoided. Although these "elevator music" collections do not contain lyrics, the melodies played will suggest the lyrics to the workshop participants and a cognitive train wreck could occur!

Bach loved food and coffee. Among his most prized possessions were his two silver coffeepots. Why not lead into the coffee break of a morning or afternoon session with the *Coffee* Cantata that Bach wrote in praise of his favorite beverage? The audience could be instructed that when the musical selection is over, so will be the break. Be careful not to use the entire cantata as break music, or the break could be longer than the work sessions.

To this point, suggestions for use of music have been limited to passive involvement. Here is a suggestion or two for active participation with music being the vehicle for learning. Have workshop groups synthesize their work by writing a song and presenting the composition to other small groups or individuals. Choose one or all of the musical creations to perform with—or for—the entire audience. The compositions can range from limericks that are said to an established drum beat, to rewritten lyrics of familiar melodies, to original compositions created for the festivities at hand. Table 9.2 is an established means of composing original songs which can serve as the medium for the message of professional development work. The music teacher can be called upon to aid in the planning of the sessions and can serve as an enabler for the composition process. All too often the music specialist is left out of the staff development loop. This is a wonderful way to increase active involvement and camaraderie among the staff.

Closing the staff development session with a song that summarizes the thoughts of the group and the developer is a memorable way to conclude the time spent together and can serve as a link to tasks to be done in the future. The lyrics of the chosen song can be part of the printed materials shared with the participants, and if singing isn't a strength of the group, at least following along and listening can inspire a continuation of shared information and implementation. The choice of music should again come from the heart of the presenter, with the ears of the participants always being considered.

Johann Sebastian Bach never expected any of his music to be published. He wrote music for an immediate purpose. He was a church organist and choir director. He needed music for every service on every Sunday, so he wrote and wrote. Some say he created 1,200 compositions (Krull, 1993, pp. 15–17). Bach did not think he was writing for posterity, but in 1977 the spacecraft *Voyager* was launched into the solar system containing three pieces by Bach, along with special record-playing equipment. Bach's work is not unlike the work of professional educators who create every day in classrooms—not for posterity, but of necessity. Who knows where an educator's creations will travel? Perhaps into the solar system and beyond!

Table 9.1
Discography for Staff Development

Bach, Johann Sebastian (1685–1750)

    Brandenberg Concertos

    Coffee Cantata

    Goldberg Variations

    Well-Tempered Clavier

The Beatles

    Beatles Anthology (1995)

Benoit, David

    Freedom at Midnight (1987)

Galway, James

    The Art of James Galway (1996)

Handel, George Frideric (1685–1759)

    Messiah (instrumental sections only)

    Water Music

Marsalis, Wynton

    In Gabriel's Garden (with the English Chamber Orchestra) (1995)

McFerrin, Bobby

    Hush (with Yo-Yo Ma) (1991)

    Paper Music (with the Saint Paul Chamber Orchestra) (1995)

Mozart, W. A. (1756–1791)

    Serenade no. 13 in G Major *(Eine Kleine Nacht Musik)*, K. 525

    Sonata for Two Pianos in D Major, K. 448

Sanborn, David

    Pearls (1995)

Scott, Tom

    Flashpoint (1988)

Vivaldi, Antonio (1678–1741)

    The Four Seasons

Table 9.2
Composing a Song

There are many different methods of writing a song. Any method is valid if it works for you. What follows is the composition technique used by the 7th- and 8th-grade general music classes in the A. MacArthur Barr Middle School, Nanuet, New York, as well as many successful professional songwriters.

The order of musical elements explored follows the sequence used in the recording studio. This strategy lends itself to organized assessment of the composition process.

Research

1. Brainstorm the work ahead by answering the following questions:
   a. What is the mood of the song to be?
   b. What message is to be conveyed through the song?
   c. Will the song contain lyrics?
   d. A hook is what is remembered most about the song. What is (are) appropriate hook(s) for this song? A hook can be found in the lyrics, melody, rhythm, etc.
2. Listen to songs that have similar qualities to the thoughts about your song and answer the following questions:
   a. What is the *form*?
   b. How is the *melody* supplied?
   c. What is the *tempo* and does it stay the same?
   d. How is the *harmony* supplied?
   e. What is the most memorable characteristic (*hook*) of the song?
   f. How are *dynamics* used to help set the mood of the song?

Apply

Use your research of other songs as a model for your song. Don't copy other artists' works, but feel free to be influenced by their work as you apply what you've learned through your research to your composition.

Create

1. If your song is to contain lyrics, write the lyrics first.
   a. Choose a song *form*. Although there are many song forms from which to choose, verse/chorus or A A B A are good beginning choices.
   b. Write the sections that are to be repeated (the chorus or A section).
   c. Write varying sections (the verses or B section).
2. Establish the *beat*, *meter*, and *rhythms* of the song. If lyrics are included, allow the lyrics to dictate the rhythm.
3. Explore and establish *harmonies* and harmonic progressions (repeated pattern of chords) to be used. Keep the progression simple! Let the chord changes be dictated by the rhythm of the lyrics.
4. Say and then sing the lyrics as the chord progression is being played. Allow a *melody* to evolve. Keep the melody simple and clear! When developing the melody, use repetition and contrast.
5. Make decisions regarding the arrangement of the music by answering the following:

Table 9.2 continued

---

   a. What instrument(s) or voice should supply the melody and harmony? (*texture*)

   b. Should there be contrast *dynamics, tempo,* and instrumentation?

   c. How long should the song be? How many times should sections be repeated?

   d. Does the song call for an introduction and/or coda?

6. Document your song through conventional means (musical notation, recording, or MIDI) or make up your own means of documentation, but be sure to document your composition. It is only through documentation that your song can be recreated by you and other performers.

Assessment

Self-assessment is a constant practice during the composition process. The composer must always make decisions regarding the composition and accept or reject each idea as appropriate for the mood and message of the song. A key question in the composition process must always be: Does it work?

4. Exemplary: Uses the conventions and rules of the modality in a highly imaginative and insightful manner.

3. Performance Standard: Effectively uses the conventions and rules of the modality to communicate.

2. Emerging: Demonstrates an attempt to use the conventions and rules of the modality but makes significant errors or has significant omissions.

1. Novice: Demonstrates a lack of awareness or understanding of the conventions and rules of the modality.

REFERENCES

Dunn, R. (1987). Research on instructional environments: Implications for student achievement and attitudes. *Professional School Psychology, 2*(1), 43–52.

Dunn, R., & Waggoner, B. (1995). Comparing three innovative instructional systems. *Emergency Librarian, 23*(1), 11–1 5.

Gremli, J. (1996). Tuned in to learning styles. *Music Educators Journal, 83*(3), 24–27.

Gremli, J., & Nicholls, L. (1994). *Practical guide to using the arts as an assessment tool.* Nanuet, NY: Nanuet Union Free School District.

Krull, K. (1993). *Lives of the musicians: Good times, bad times (and what the neighbors thought).* San Diego: Harcourt, Brace, Jovanovich.

Lozanov, G. (1978). *Suggestology and outlines of suggestopedy.* London: Gordon and Breach.

Pizzo, J., Dunn, R., and Dunn, K. (1990, July/September). A sound approach to reading: Responding to students' learning styles. *Journal of Reading, Writing and Learning Disabilities International, 6*(3), 249–260.

Rauscher, F., Shaw, G., & Ky, K. (1993). Music and special task performance. *Nature, 365,* 611.

10

Using Programmed Learning Sequences: Step by Step!

Roger Callan

Let me tell you a story about a young person who was the nicest guy you would ever want to meet. His mother thought the world of him; his father bored his colleagues at the office about his accomplishments. Even his sister grudgingly consented to the opinion that he was "nice" sometimes. In fact, virtually everyone who knew him liked him and admired him. A teacher might well say: "Now that's a boy I would like to have in my classroom."

Would you?

Mike was great in sports, making model airplanes, helping out at home, taking care of the baby. But in school, there was what can be delicately described as a problem. Mike could not understand what the teacher was talking about most of the time. That is a problem when most teachers just love to talk to kids. Explanations are often verbal, directions verbal, new information verbal, and reinforcement verbal. If, like Mike (or Martha), a student is not able to listen and take in all that, then problems result. Certainly his attention span was pretty short when the teacher talked beyond a few minutes. "Michael, are you paying attention?" was a familiar refrain in his classes.

Yet Mike could build sometimes stunning model jet planes and even help his dad out around the house with electrical and plumbing problems, which his dad appreciated very much, constantly telling him what a great job he was doing and that he admired the way Mike could follow the steps in the direction booklet or manuals that they both used. Mike loved hearing that and feeling his dad's hand on his shoulder. He was doing something that was appreciated and was being told that in no uncertain terms. You name it—that kid was not stupid. Then what was the problem?

His teacher knew that too, but that didn't help matters. Miss Carmody would try and explain new material to Mike several times in different ways to try and get the point across. That didn't work. She tried getting other good students to demonstrate the same thing and show Mike how to do math problems, history projects, science tasks, but again there was no growth, no moment of insight. Miss Carmody was as frustrated as her students, especially since Mike was such a great guy and seemed so able.

One day there was a crisis at school. All the lights went out and all the devices dependent on electricity went dead. The kids, taking a sensible view of the situation, went berserk. Teachers were frantic trying to calm them down and wondered themselves what was going on and what would happen. The principal, Mrs. Simon, came into Miss Carmody's classroom. She asked the teacher, in a voice the kids could hear, if she had any experience with things electrical, as Mr. Carmody was well known as the most reliable electrician in town. Poor Miss Carmody didn't have a clue about such things: "My husband sees to all that," she said desperately. Mike overheard that, though, and volunteered to help. Mrs. Simon looked at the diminutive nine-year-old unbelievingly when he said: "My dad and I fixed the primary circuits to the washer-dryer last week, taking care not to get the 120 and 240 voltages mixed up. It was simple—one wire had slipped out of a circuit breaker. We'd never seen anything like that before, but it was easy to fix." A short, stunned silence followed this remark, and then Mrs. Simon said smartly, "Come with me, young man," and off she led the glowing Mike into areas students were forbidden to enter. In the basement of the school, the darkness was broken by an emergency light which cast dark shadows over everything. "The caretaker is away looking after his mother," Mrs. Simon explained, "and I've been here long enough to have learned something about all these things. But I've never done them myself. Here is the manual for such things." She showed Mike a giant loose-leaf folder. "We will have to walk our way through all this together."

As it turned out, Mrs. Simon just stood there as Mike, taking each little instruction at a time, traced his way through wires and circuit breakers (all safely neutralized) under Mrs. Simon's eagle but amazed eye. The manual had broken everything down into simple steps, each with a diagram which looked exactly like the content of the wall box. There was even a continuity tester (powered by nothing more threatening than a AA battery) which allowed Mike to see if what he was doing was correct, step by step. All through this, Mrs. Simon could see that he was doing exactly what the manual said, and she complimented him through it all. Mike loved it: here was the principal of the school saying what a great job he was doing, how the whole school would be proud of him, how she was amazed at his ability to translate from the book to a real-life situation, and so on.

"Right," he said at last. "That should be it. Switch on." It was not without some trepidation that Mrs. Simon turned the switch, but the lights came on and the computers glowed again. Mike had saved the day. And this was accomplished by a student the teachers had all despaired over.

Something was wrong. Mrs. Simon began to retrace the events in the basement. Mike had worked diligently, reading a sentence at a time, checking everything with the diagrams and the tester, going back to the previous entry if the tester did not light up to show that a circuit had connected, and exclaiming with pleasure every time the device did light up. This little fellow could triumph over all the odds if, it seemed to her, it was broken into small steps, with some kind of reinforcement to confirm that what he was doing was right. "I wonder if I've stumbled onto something," she thought.

Indeed she had. She had found the secret behind the Programmed Learning Sequence, or PLS, a learning tool for a certain type of learner. This chapter introduces you to a learning tool which helps students who

- have a short attention span
- tend to be visual and tactual
- need immediate reinforcement
- have a high need for sequenced structured learning
- learn in small increments

QUESTION: How was the concept of a Programmed Learning Sequence (PLS) introduced to you in this chapter? (Try to answer this before reading on; the answer will be provided below so that you can self-correct. Try to do this for every question as it comes up: decide on an answer and then read on to see if you were correct. If you were not, then look back over the previous text to see where you went wrong and why.)

ANSWER: The PLS was introduced to you through a story.

This is a "global" way of introducing any new and difficult learning for certain types of youngsters—those who are motivated by anecdotes, stories, pictures, color, and fantasy. The story includes the essential elements of the new learning; therefore, it mentioned that Mike lacked a long attention span, but could read and follow diagrams or pictures very well. This meant that he tended to be a visual learner, someone who remembers much of what he sees. He was also able to make great-looking model planes with his own hands and liked to have his father give reinforcement to what he was doing. This suggests someone who learns through his hands—a tactual learner. When these characteristics are present, learning takes place for this type of student. After being motivated, many analytic students, those who are sequential and persistent and prefer learning from the first step to the last, also benefit from Programmed Learning Sequences.

Students with a tactual preference for learning will often excel in those subjects which require hands-on experience. Therefore, chemistry laboratory work will be exciting and rewarding for them. Art is frequently a very stimulating experience for them as they create colors and designs from their experience. The challenge for teachers in the other subjects, of course, is to figure out a way to translate their work into something such students can actually see or feel. For example, if this book were entirely devoted to presenting the PLS and its structure, what shape would be appropriate, provided that the printers could make a book into any shape imaginable? Perhaps a "lamp of learning" shape would suggest what it is about. "Tall tales" would be long and slim; "the world" would be round with hemispheres on the cover. Whatever shape is appropriate, the student will have the same message conveyed in two different ways, namely, the text and the shape of the page on which the text is written. Students will be able to see and feel the learning they are reading. In this regard, texture, wraparounds, and shape-coded task cards can be added to certain frames for tactual reinforcement.

QUESTION: What is an appropriate way to present a PLS?

ANSWER: The best way to present a PLS is to create a shape consonant with the material being presented.

Hence if you were to do a PLS on the topic of space exploration, then the space shuttle would be a suitable shape (see Figure 10.1). A topic on the 13 colonies might be in the shape of a map of the east coast of North America in the 18th century, and so on. Something is learned the first time the student sets eyes on the PLS because of its shape, title, color, diagram, art work, and so forth.

A PLS is divided into several pages called frames. Each frame contains just one important concept or fact or essential idea concerning the topic. It is important also to try and find a suitable drawing or photograph which complements the idea, so that a visual image reinforces the text of the frame. The text should be in a language readily understandable to students, and it aids the learning process if the fact or concept is repeated in several ways so that students really can get a grasp on the concept. Then, very important, at the end of each frame a single question is posed to students. This should be based on the central idea of the text, the idea that the

Figure 10.1

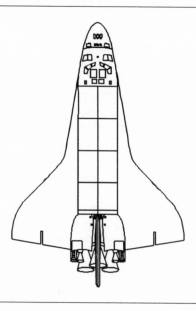

frame is seeking to impart. Answers should be required in a variety of ways. For example, fill in; circle the right answer; draw an arrow to the right pair of responses; underline the correct response; highlight the right answer; and so forth.

QUESTION: What should each frame of a PLS contain?

ANSWER: In Figure 10.2, the frame of the PLS demonstrates only one concept or thought concerning the topic, reinforced with graphics, to make it clear and understandable to students.

Students for whom the PLS is a good learning tool also like to be entertained when they are studying. Teachers know that the heaviest topic can be lightened with anecdotal stories or some light jokes. Such an approach helps some students understand the topic better. This should also be reflected in the frames of the PLS. Humor is a good ally to have in learning and should be used when appropriate, especially when reinforcing an important point. It is therefore recommended that the answer to the question at the end of each frame, which provides immediate feedback to the student, should be accompanied with a few well-chosen words and/or a graphic to make the student feel good.

QUESTION: What should accompany the answer to the question at the end of each frame in a PLS?

ANSWER: Each answer should have some humorous graphic or comment attached which reinforces the new learning.

Figure 10.2

Each frame of the PLS, then, contains a single concept, followed by a question, which is to be completed by the student and checked immediately for the correct response on the back of each frame. Graphics and humorous comments may also accompany this information. This pattern continues for a series of frames, perhaps four or five. Then, because of short attention span of the student for whom this is an appropriate learning tool, a reinforcement exercise is recommended, a kind of review test on the recently learned material. It should concern itself only with the sequence of frames just read, nothing more. It should also be constructed in a tactual mode, for example, task cards, tucked into an envelope on the frame, with the question on one end of the card, and the answer on the other, each cut in a unique way so that no other answer can fit to the question. Therefore, the "test" is self-correcting and fun to do at the same time. The student is able also to return to the previous frames to find out the answers if they cannot be remembered, thereby enhancing the possibility of retention even more. An electroboard, pic-a-hole, or other tactual resource (as explained elsewhere in this book) are also acceptable ways of reinforcing the recently learned material.

> QUESTION: What should follow a sequence of about four or five frames in a PLS?

> ANSWER: A summative type of reinforcement exercise presented in a tactual format. Figure 10.3 provides examples of three task cards based on the work so far in this chapter.

Figure 10.4 contains some further examples of task cards with the question on one side and the answer on the other, based on what this chapter has said about PLSs so far. Each task card should be cut into two pieces, but each card should be cut in a different way so that only those two halves can fit together correctly.

The PLS contains several objectives selected by the teacher as the most important in the particular topic selected. A typical number of objectives would be about seven or eight, though the number may vary depending on the topic, difficulty, level of ability of the students, degree of sophistication, and so on. These objectives would be identical to those chosen for the Contract Activity Package (explained in Chapter 11). The PLS should contain a few of the tactual resources explained in other chapters to reinforce learning. These objectives contain the essential elements

Figure 10.3

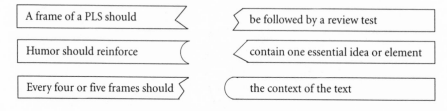

Figure 10.4

What content should be found on a frame in a PLS?	A single, important fact or concept, graphics, and a concluding question based on the text of that frame with a space for answers
What type of learner will benefit most from a PLS?	A student who has a short attention span, is sequential, visual, and tactual, and requires immediate reinforcement
What is the objective of placing a question at the end of a frame and the answer following on the next frame?	To provide immediate reinforcement for the new learning and to allow the student to self-correct

required by the student to master the new learning. For example, the objectives of this chapter on the PLS to be mastered by you, the reader, would be:

1. The type of student for whom the PLS is a recommended technique
2. The shape of a PLS
3. The global introduction
4. The layout and contents of a frame
5. The rationale and use of graphics and tactual materials
6. The importance of immediate feedback and positive reinforcement
7. The frequency of summative learning exercises

QUESTION: What gives the structure to a PLS; on what is it based?

ANSWER: The PLS is based on a series of objectives selected by the teacher which contain the essential elements or ideas of the new learning. Just like the hours in the day, the PLS plays through a sequenced list of objectives so that new learning is acquired. The frames should increase in difficulty as the student progresses through the PLS.

The text should be uncomplicated and clear. The PLS is designed for a slower-learning youngster, and so the text should be set at a level which the student is able to comprehend without stress. Naturally this will vary depending on the grade level and ability of the student. Care should be taken that the language is neither too advanced nor too simple, but set as close to the reading ability level of the student as possible. Some students may have difficulty reading anything at all, and the teacher should compensate for this by recording the text of the PLS on a cassette which the student can listen to while going through the PLS. In this way, the student follows the text in the PLS and also hears the text being read by the teacher. The recording also instructs the student on what to do. For example, the student will be told to press the "pause" button on the cassette recorder after the question at the end of a frame in order to give him or her a chance to determine the answer.

QUESTION: What consideration should be given to the language of the PLS text?

ANSWER: The PLS language should be carefully geared to the reading level of the students using the PLS. (After all, the idea is that the students understand what you're saying. Isn't it?)

Finally, the brighter students who prefer working with the PLS strategy should be challenged to create new ones for use with other students. They will learn even more by designing ones with correct responses based on resources they are required to locate. They will gain confidence and improved self-image through pride of authorship and recognition.

Using Contract Activity Packages: A CAP-ital Idea!

Rose Frances Lefkowitz

Another staff development lecture is about to take place at the school called ISN, nicknamed the "Ignore Staff Needs" High School. Nancy the Nonconformist and Gloria the Gifted are two teachers headed down the hall to the lecture. Nancy says, "I am going under protest! I do not want to go to this." Gloria says, "I agree. I have too much to do. And I get nothing out of this type of session anyway." They both take front row seats next to each other. As the high-priced consultant begins to lecture at the front of the room, they doze off about 10 minutes into the presentation. Insulted, Carl the consultant stops and walks over to the teachers. He taps Gloria on the shoulder. "Am I boring you?" he questions. Gloria retorts, "The subject matter could be interesting if presented in the right way to me." "How?" asks the consultant as he throws the cap he is holding into the air. Gifted Gloria grabs it. "That's it!" she shouts. I would like to do a CAP—Contract Activity Package—where multisensory activities would stimulate and retain my interest." Nancy snaps back into reality, hears the suggestion, stands up from her seat, and shouts, "What a "CAP-ital idea!"

"What is a CAP?" queries Carl the consultant. Gifted Gloria takes the podium and begins to explain. During this session, we will construct a CAP that can be utilized for virtually any topic on staff development. Let's begin!

NAME OF CONTRACT ACTIVITY PACKAGE: CONTRACT ACTIVITY PACK-
AGE (CAP) FOR STAFF DEVELOPMENT OR "CAP"ITALIZING ON THE
DEVELOPMENT OF STAFF. WHAT A "CAP"ITAL IDEA!

PARTICIPANT'S NAME:_____

DEPARTMENT/DIVISION:_____

DATE THE CAP WAS BEGUN: _____

DATE THE CAP WAS COMPLETED: _____

ACTIVITY ALTERNATIVES SELECTED: _____

_____

_____

_____

_____

_____

_____

REPORTING ALTERNATIVES SELECTED: _____

_____

_____

_____

_____

_____

_____

PARTICIPANT'S POST-TEST ASSESSMENT:_____

NAMES OF PARTICIPANTS THAT
WORKED AS A TEAM ON THIS
CONTRACT ACTIVITY PACKAGE: _____

_____

_____

_____

_____

INTRODUCTION

Dear Participants:

This is a Contract Activity Package (CAP) designed to teach you how to understand and use a CAP for any staff development topic area. It is an individualized educational plan that will facilitate your learning. You may work on it alone, with a friend, or as part of a team through the small group activities that are included.

This CAP is organized into five (5) sections each with a different instructional goal called a *behavioral objective*. For each objective, these *resource alternatives* provide many options through which you are able to teach yourself what has to be learned.

At the end of this CAP, you will find a list of resources that will help you to learn all that is required. These include journals, books, and participant-made tactile/kinesthetic materials.

To demonstrate that you have learned the objective you may select among several *activity alternatives* and their companion *reporting alternatives* for each of the five instructional goals. Each of the *activity alternatives* is designed to appeal to a major perceptual strength: auditory, visual, tactual, or kinesthetic. Completing these also reinforces the knowledge gained; teaching the material doubly reinforces what is learned and helps others, too.

If you need any further assistance in working with this CAP, please do not hesitate in consulting with your coordinator of staff development activities. Good luck!

BEHAVIORAL OBJECTIVE 1: become familiar with the basic components of a CAP.

(a) clearly stated objectives that begin with a verb

(b) an analytic and global title (with humor, if possible)

(c) multisensory activity and reporting alternatives

(d) multisensory resource alternatives

(e) at least three (3) small-group techniques

(f) assessment directly related to objectives

(g) multiple, related illustrations; color

(h) humor related to the objectives, concept, activities

(i) neatness; attractiveness; legibility

(j) spelling and grammar correct

(k) original, creative

(l) related to participants' interests; life style; or talents

(m) interdisciplinary, if possible

(n) offers some participant choices

(o) includes coordinator/participant-made tactual instructional alternatives

(p) includes tape for participants who retain information through auditory modality

"Capitalize on your strengths"

Complete at least two (2) of the Activity and Reporting Alternatives in this section. Remember, if you need help, refer to the Resource List at the back of the CAP.

Activity Alternatives	**Reporting Alternatives**
1. Create a crossword puzzle using key words of the basic components of a CAP.	1. Let other participants try to complete it. Check and return their answers to them.
2. Create a set of ten (10) task cards which include the basic components of a CAP.	2. Choose two (2) participants to reassemble your task cards.
3. Create a floor game using the list of the basic components of a CAP.	3. Play the game with a group of participants.
4. Write a letter to a friend describing the basic components of a CAP.	4. Choose at least three (3) participants to read your letter.
5. Tape record a speech of approximately 10 minutes in which you persuade the U.S. Senate to fund the creation of staff development CAPs for every faculty member in the U.S.	5. Play the tape for five teachers. Ask for suggestions to improve it. Mail it to your favorite Senator.

BEHAVIORAL OBJECTIVE 2: identify the purpose of each of the basic components of a CAP.

component: clearly stated objectives that begin with a verb

purpose: knowing what is expected is important to participant motivation; specific knowledge that is worthwhile to master is indicated by clear objectives prompted by a verb toward action activities.

component: analytic and global title (with humor)

purpose: participants process and retain information in different ways; analytics prefer a straightforward title that indicates the subject matter being presented; globals prefer a lighter title, with humor, relating the subject matter in a clever way; titles must be introduced both ways to "cap"ture the attention of global participants as well as analytic processors.

component: multisensory activity and reporting alternatives

purpose: a series of creative activities through which the participant demonstrates that the information has been mastered; activity alternatives should include all four perceptual strengths: auditory, visual, tactual, or kinesthetic in format; multisensory options are provided that match perceptual strength and learning style; participants engaged in creative activity want to share with peers; reporting alternatives allowing the participant to share reinforces subject matter and increases retention of material.

component: multisensory resource alternatives

purpose: participants are given a list of available resources that may be used to learn the information as required by their objectives; resources are multisensory in nature, appealing to participants' perceptual strength and learning style.

component: at least three (3) small group techniques

purpose: these techniques are included in a CAP to allow participants, according to their learning style preferences, to work in small groups or pairs to master difficult objectives together rather than by themselves; instructional peer learning strategy.

component: assessment directly related to objectives

purpose: the post-test assessment for participants identifies how much of the information required by the behavioral objectives the participant has already mastered and how much remains to be learned; having the test before one begins builds confidence; the participant knows what is expected.

component: multiple, related illustrations; color

purpose: the addition of related illustrations and color gives the participant a heightened sense of the subject matter being introduced; they aid in maintaining interest.

component: humor related to the objectives, concept, activities

purpose: smiles and laughter will "cap"ture the attention of the global participants to the subject matter being introduced; most of the participants in the audience process information globally; many analytics enjoy humor too—especially word and number references.

component: neatness; attractiveness; legibility

purpose: professionalism through typeface, spacing, and visual appeal is important so that participants would be more willing to try it compared to many manuals they are given.

component: spelling and grammar correct

purpose: participants will appreciate the material that maintains high standards.

component: original; creative

purpose: participants have an opportunity to develop multisensory activities for learning purposes; the participant gets a sense of accomplishment.

component: related to participants' interests; life styles; or talents

purpose: participants will be motivated through how the CAP relates to their interests and preferences while learning.

component: interdisciplinary, if possible

purpose: will have opportunities to see relationships between and among different disciplines; also participants from different subject areas will be able to work together and learn from each other.

component: offers some participant choices

purpose: some participants prefer choices while learning new material; options motivate many participants.

component: includes coordinator/participant-made tactual instructional materials

purpose: participant can engage in related instructional devices to reinforce subject material being presented.

component: tape for participants who prefer the auditory modality

purpose: to provide the tape for those whose perceptual strength is through auditory means.

Let the CAP  **point you in the right direction!**

Complete at least three (3) of the Activity and Reporting Alternatives.

Activity Alternatives

1. Make a transparency indicating the purpose of each of the basic components of a CAP.

2. Make an audiotape describing the purpose of each of the basic components of a CAP.

3. Perform a videotape depicting a question and answer discussion on the purpose of each of the components of a CAP.

4. Using small group technique, select five (5) participants and go to the microcomputer lab. Brain-storm on all the basic components of a CAP and their purposes. Recorder should enter the data on the computer.

5. Circle of knowledge
   Turn to the next page for information and directions for this activity and its reporting alternative.

Reporting Alternatives

1. Display your transparency on an overhead projector to a group of three (3) participants.

2. Have a small group of friends listen to the tape for review of the topic.

3. Have a pair (2) of participants view the videotape discussion.

4. Select five (5) other participants to assess the results and share printouts of the information with the participants.

5. **Activity Alternative**

CIRCLE OF KNOWLEDGE: This is another small group technique that you may select to help you learn the basic components of a CAP and their purposes. This is sure to make Gifted Gloria proud of you!

Procedure: Position several small circles of chairs (4 to 5 in a group) evenly about the room. One participant in each group should be appointed or elected as a group recorder. (Use a humorous method of selection, e.g. curliest hair, lives farthest away and so forth.) One question is posed that will have many possible answers. Each circle of knowledge team will respond to the same question simultaneously. A member in each group will be designated as first to begin and then answers are provided by one member at a time going around the circle. A recorder writes down the responses after a predetermined time period.

Reporting Alternative: At the end of this period, the responses of both groups can be compared and the group with the most correct responses wins!

Circle Members:

1._____   4._____

2._____   5._____

3._____

Recorder_____

The Question: List and identify as many of the basic components of a CAP and their purposes as you can.

Five (5) minute time limit.

1._____

_____

2._____

_____

3._____

_____

4._____

_____

5._____

_____

6._____

_____

7._____

_____

8._____

_____

9._____

_____

10._____

_____

11._____

_____

12._____

_____

13._____

_____

14._____

_____

15._____

_____

16._____

_____

BEHAVIORAL OBJECTIVE 3: describe the learning style traits of participants for whom a CAP is likely to be effective.

Complete number 3 (Team Learning) and one other Activity and Reporting Alternative.

Activity Alternatives

1. Make an audiotape describing the learning style traits of participants for whom a CAP is likely to be effective.

2. Using the chapter on CAPs in the text *Teaching Elementary/Secondary Students Through Their Individual Learning Styles* by Drs. Rita and Kenneth Dunn as a reference, construct a pic-a-hole on this subject.

3. Team Learning
   Turn to the next page for information and directions for this activity.

4. Create a floor game based on a sporting event that describes the learning style strengths of participants for whom a CAP is likely to be effective.

Reporting Alternatives

1. Lend this tape to other participants for home study.

2. Test the knowledge of another group of participants using the pic-a-hole cards on this topic.

3. Have at least four (4) teams compare answers. Let a "jury" select the best responses.

4. Have four (4) participants play the game. Keep score and award a prize.

TEAM LEARNING is an excellent small group technique to learn new material. To get involved, form at least four (4) groups of four (4) to five (5) participants and arrange seats in a circle or find any seating that is comfortable for the group. When comfortable, each group should elect one member to act as recorder, a person who will write the group's responses. Use humorous "selection" procedures as indicated for circle of knowledge. Read the information on the following page describing those participants for whom a CAP would likely be effective. Or, listen to the audiotape of it. Then, as a group, answer the questions posed on the next page. Any member may help other participants on the same team, but all effort must be concentrated within the group and the group must come to a consensus. Twenty (20) minutes are allowed for the completion of the team learning. The facilitator will then ask each recorder, in turn, the answers to the questions, and write these answers on the board or overhead projection transparency. The team that has the most correct answers will get a free pizza and soda!

TEAM LEARNING

Team Members

1._____

2._____

3._____

4._____

5._____

6._____

Please turn to the next page for the information describing those participants for whom a CAP is most likely to be effective.

PARTICIPANTS FOR WHOM A CAP IS MOST LIKELY EFFECTIVE

CAPs are best for motivated, auditory, or visual learners; also, they are responsive to nonconformists because of the many options available. Gloria the Gifted and Nancy the Nonconformist love to learn new and difficult material by designing a contract activity package (CAP).

The CAP permits participants to work either alone, with another participant or two, or as part of a team through small group activities that are included.

The Resource Alternatives section of the CAP includes auditory, visual, and tactual or kinesthetic resources permitting participants to learn through their strongest perceptual strength and to reinforce what they've learned through a secondary perceptual strength.

The CAP may be used anytime—during the early morning hours, after dinner—to match the individual learner's best time of day for concentrating and producing. No more dozing off during staff development lectures for Gloria and Nancy. They can master the staff development subject matter through a CAP at any time of day or night.

Participants who work on a CAP may adjust for light, temperature, and design to match their learning style characteristics for those elements.

Choice is an important feature of the CAP. Participants who prefer options will find working with the CAP most accommodating to their learning style traits.

Complete the following questions as a group letting your recorder write down the answers:

1. CAPs are best for what type of participants? _____

_____

2. The CAP permits participants to work alone, or _____

_____

3. The Resource Alternatives section of the CAP includes which senses to permit participants to learn through their strongest perceptual strength? _____

_____

4. At what time of day or night may the participant use the CAP to learn new or difficult staff development concepts? _____

_____

5. Do the learning style characteristics of light, temperature, design have an impact on those participants working on a CAP? _____

_____

6. What is an important feature of the CAP that accommodates participants' learning styles? _____

_____

7. How could CAPs be used in the military? in professional sports? in Congress? in college teaching? _____

_____

8. What are some advantages of CAPs that are not listed in any answers above? ___

_____

9. Create a tactual strategy or kinesthetic game to teach participants for whom CAPs are effective.

BEHAVIORAL OBJECTIVE 4: design effective strategies for introducing and involving diverse groups in using a CAP.

Complete at least two (2) of the Activity and Reporting Alternatives.

Activity Alternatives	Reporting Alternatives
1. Create a list of all members of the staff and their area of expertise on in-service presentations. Have each member create a CAP on his or her area of expertise.	1. During brown bag in-service sessions (scheduled during lunch hour), have each member on a rotating basis present his or her CAP each week.
2. Gather senior staff members who are willing to form a teacher mentoring program designed to encourage and assist new staff on constructing and implementing the CAP on specific assigned staff development issues.	2. Staff members report on the process of constructing a CAP and orally present staff development issues through the CAP format at weekly scheduled workshops.
3. Have staff members do a library search or have them refer to the publications in the Resource List of this CAP. Draft a synopsis of the staff development issues of the article or books read, and put into a CAP format to overcome problems and have the staff move forward.	3. Share developed CAPs on staff development issues with other members of the school at times of day or night according to their individual preferences.
4. Design a giant electroboard for the teachers' room which "keeps score" on what teachers want to learn.	4. Have a team of teachers prepare reports and tallies for use in planning staff development.
5. Create a floor game that teachers can play which would promote alternate strategies to conduct staff development.	5. Appoint referees to conduct the game and register recommendations.

BEHAVIORAL OBJECTIVE 5: list three (3) advantages and three (3) disadvantages of using CAPs in staff development.

Complete at least two (2) Activity and Reporting Alternatives.

Activity Alternatives

1. Make an audiotape explaining three (3) advantages and three (3) disadvantages of using a CAP in staff development.

2. Make a poster outlining three (3) advantages and three (3) disadvantages of using CAPs in staff development.

3. Utilizing the group analysis technique, turn to the next page for information.

4. Videotape a twelve (12) to twenty (20) minute film depicting advantages, disadvantages and how to overcome the latter.

5. Design a board game that describes advantages and disadvantages.

6. Create a walking tour through horrors of staff development to the praise of learning.

Reporting Alternatives

1. Have a small group of participants listen to the tape.

2. Display the poster on the wall of the staff development seminar room.

3. Compare responses with three (3) other groups.

4. Show the film to a group of teachers for suggestions.

5. Play the game with five (5) teachers.

6. Take six (6) teachers on the tour.

GROUP ANALYSIS

Group Members' Names:

1. _____ 3. _____

2. _____ 4. _____

1. List the three (3) advantages of using a CAP in staff development.

2. List the three (3) disadvantages of using a CAP in staff development.

At the end of the group analysis session, Gloria the Gifted turns to Carl the consultant and says, "Now, you are ready to be tested. Let's see what you've learned about the CAP and staff development." Carl replies to Gloria, "I am ready to be tested. However, who was giving consultation to whom?"

RESOURCES

Participant-Made Resources

These are located in the Multisensory Instructional Package (MIP). For directions on how to use these refer to the last pages of the script for the MIP.

- Learning Circle
- Task Cards
- Pic-A-Hole
- Flip Chute
- Electroboard
- Tape Recording of Programmed Learning Sequence
- Tape Recording of Contract Activity Package Script
- Tape Recording of MIP Script
- Staff Development Floor Game

Books

Beattie, M. (1995). *Constructing Professional Knowledge in Teaching.* Teachers College Press, 1234 Amsterdam Avenue, New York, New York 10027.

Bradley, H. (1991). *Staff Development.* The Falmer Press, 4 John Street, London WCIN 2ET.

Dunn, R., & Dunn, K. (1992). *Teaching Elementary Students Through Their Individual Learning Styles.* Allyn & Bacon, Simon & Schuster, Inc., 160 Gould Street, Needham Heights, Massachusetts 02194.

Dunn, R., & Dunn, K. (1993). *Teaching Secondary Students Through Their Individual Learning Styles.* Allyn & Bacon, Simon & Schuster, Inc., 160 Gould Street, Needham Heights, Massachusetts 02194.

Grimmett, P., & Neufeld, J. (1994). *Teacher Development and the Struggle for Authenticity.* Teachers College Press, 1234 Amsterdam Avenue, New York, New York 10027.

Hargreaves, A., & Fullan, M. (1992). *Understanding Teacher Development.* Teachers College Press, Columbia University, New York, New York 10027.

Houston-Woods, M., & Haskell, J. & Lawler, P. (1990). *Staff Development: The Key to School Renewal.* Research for Better Schools, 444 North Third Street, Philadelphia, PA 19123.

Joyce, B. (1990). *Changing School Culture through Staff Development.* Alexandria, VA: Association for Supervision and Curriculum Development.

Lieberman, A., & Miller, L. (1991). *Staff Development for Education in the 90's.* Teachers College Press, Columbia University, New York, New York 10027.

Richardson, V. (1994). *Teacher Change and the Staff Development Process.* Teachers College Press, Columbia University, New York, New York 10027.

Williams, M. (1991). *In-service Education and Training.* Cassell Educational Limited, Villiers House, 41/47 Strand, London WC2N 5JE.

Journals

Allen, B. (1992). A Case Study in Planning Staff Development. *American Annals of the Deaf. 139*(5), 493–499.

Asayesh, G. (1994, Winter). Effective Advocacy for Staff Development. *Journal of Staff Development, 15*(1), 52–55.

Dunn, K., Dunn, R., & Freeley, M.E. (1985, April). Tips to Improve Your Inservice Training. *Early Years/K-8,* 30–31.

Dunn, R., Griggs, S., Olson, J., Beasley, M., & Gorman, B. (1995, July/August). A Meta-Analytic Validation of the Dunn and Dunn Model of Learning Style Preferences. *Journal of Educational Research, 88*(6), 353–362.

Filipczak, B. (1995, March). Different Strokes: Learning Styles in the Classroom. *Training,* 43–48.

Filipczak, B. (1995, May). Out of the Can: How to Customize Off-the-Shelf Training. *Training,* 51–55

Fullan, M. (1993, March). Why Teachers Must Become Change Agents. *Educational Leadership,* 12–15.

Gallegos, J. (1994, Fall). Staff Development Strategies That Facilitate a Transition in Educational Paradigms. *Journal of Staff Development, 15*(4), 34–38.

Guskey, T. (1994, Fall). Results-oriented Professional Development: In Search of an Optimal Mix of Effective Practices. *Journal of Staff Development, 15*(4), 42–50.

Hequet, M. (1995). Quality Goes to School. *Training,* 47–54.

Higgins, J. (1994, November). Training 101: Creating Creativity. *Training and Development,* 11–15.

Joyce, B. (1993, Summer). Four Responses to Orlich and Others. *Journal of Staff Development, 14*(3), 10–17.

Joyce, B., & Calhoun, E. (1995, April). School Renewal: An Inquiry, Not a Formula. *Educational Leadership,* 51–55.

Knoll, M. (1993). Staff Development: Content, Process, Transfer. *NYC Challenge,* 15–19.

Lieberman, A. (1995, April). Practices that Support Teacher Development. *Phi Delta Kappan,* 591–596.

McBride, R., Reed, J., & Dollar, J. (1994, Spring). Teacher Attitudes Toward Staff Development: A Symbolic Relationship at Best. *Journal of Staff Development, 15*(2), 36–41.

Michalko, M. (1994, June). Bright Ideas. *Training and Development,* 44–47.

Miranda-Halsell, A., & Scott, J. (1994, Summer). Preparing Classroom Teachers for the Future: The Development, Implementation and Follow-up of a Multicultural Education Course. *Journal of Staff Development, 15*(3), 50–53.

Rudolph, S., & Preston, L. (1995, September). Teaching Teachers. *The Science Teacher,* 30–32.

Showers, B. (1990, May/June). Aiming for Superior Classroom Instruction for All Children: A Comprehensive Staff Development Model. *Remedial and Special Education, 11*(3), 35–39.

Showers, B., Joyce, B., & Bennett, B. (1987, November). Synthesis of Research on Staff Development: A Framework for Future Study and a State-of-the-Art analysis. *Educational Leadership,* 77–87.

Sparks, D. (1994, Fall). A Paradigm Shift in Staff Development. *Journal of Staff Development, 15*(4), 26–29.

Sparks, D. (1994, Winter). Staff Development Implications of National Board Certification: An Interview with NBPTS's James Smith. *Journal of Staff Development, 15*(1), 58–59.

Sparks, D., & Vaughn, S. (1994, Spring). What Every School Board Member Should Know About Staff Development. *Journal of Staff Development 15*(2), 20–22.

Todnem, G., & Warner, M. (1994, Fall). The QUILT Program Assesses Teacher and Student Change. *Journal of Staff Development, 15*(4), 66–67.

Equipment

Microcomputer laboratory.

PARTICIPANT'S NAME

POST-TEST ASSESSMENT

Questions 1 to 16 focus on the basic components of the Contract Activity Package (CAP) and their related purposes. Fill in the corresponding information requested on this concept.

Components of CAPs	Purpose
1. _____	_____
2. _____	_____
3. _____	_____
4. _____	_____
5. _____	_____
6. _____	_____
7. _____	_____
8. _____	_____
9. _____	_____
10. _____	_____
11. _____	_____
12. _____	_____
13. _____	_____
14. _____	_____
15. _____	_____
16. _____	_____

17. Describe the learning style traits of participants for whom a CAP is likely to be effective.

_____

_____

_____

18. Name the feasible strategies for introducing and involving diverse groups in using a CAP.

_____

_____

_____

19. Based upon your readings on the resource list, cite three (3) advantages of using CAPs in staff development.

   _____

   _____

   _____

20. Based upon your readings on the resource list, cite three (3) disadvantages of using CAPs in staff development.

   _____

   _____

   _____

Using Tactual Instructional Resources: Hands On!

Roger Callan

The means whereby information is taken into our minds, according to the research, varies with each individual. Some of us easily remember and understand instructions and new learning simply by hearing it explained and presented well. Others of us recall information which we have read and seen illustrated or demonstrated to us. Still others of us love visiting new places and learning through experiencing novel situations, as if learning through our whole bodies.

The learning this chapter is going to examine concerns those of us who learn through another way, by "hands-on" experience. These are the people who excel in situations such as laboratory experiments and workshop-type subjects. They are handy about the house and can generally fix things with the greatest of ease. They are the people who love to make model airplanes, ships, and cars and who can impress their friends by manual dexterity. It seems, therefore, that such people learn through their hands, demonstrating a "tactual" learning.

The challenge for any teacher of such people, of course, is how to teach them through their dominant learning strength. Are there ways in which educational objectives usually taught through traditional approaches such as lecture and assigned reading can be attained through purely tactual techniques? If teachers have students who are primarily tactual learners, which means that more traditional teaching techniques such as reading and listening to the teacher do not work very well for them, how can conscientious teachers ensure that such students learn with the same success as all other students? That is a challenge for teachers, especially if they do not even know which, if any, of their students are tactual learners. Frequently, many students diagnosed as special education students are strongly tactual learners. Given the opportunity to learn in a tactual way, many times they can compete successfully with mainstreamed students. Teachers who have experienced such success with students who have been traditionally assigned to the lowest tracks in school see the efficacy of such techniques and how worthwhile they are.

The tactual techniques which are going to be described and explained here are very simple to create and use, easy to learn, and in many cases responsible for breakthroughs in learning for strongly tactual young people for whom academic success has been elusive. The techniques are perhaps deceptively simple and are open to ridicule from people who are not tactual learners. For such nontactual learners, it is probably inconceivable that anyone could learn in ways so different from their own. The research findings do not agree with them, however, and teachers who have tried these techniques know for a fact that they work with students who learn tactually.

One suggestion to new practitioners is to begin using these techniques with a unit which, in your experience, has been traditionally a great challenge to students. There is no real point in making tactual materials in a unit which students have always found easy to understand. Instead, make tactual materials for the unit which has the greatest challenge for your students in the year, where you may be desperate for any help and grateful for any new approach. That is the area in which you should begin using these materials.

TASK CARDS

Let us begin with a technique which most students, no matter how they learn, know very well: task cards. These are simply cards with crucial information or key facts or principles which must be known in the unit of knowledge under study. Examples would be dates of important events in history; chemical equations for important reactions; drama plot development scenes for English; and so on. Normal task cards are simple, basic building blocks for any subject, and they usually appear just before examinations. These cards can easily be transformed into tactual learning materials.

For example, you have a task card in historical exploration, and a question is created in that area, such as: What was the great incentive for exploring westward across an uncharted Atlantic Ocean in the late 15th century? The answer is: The lure of enormous financial profit in finding a cheaper way of getting silks, spices, and other produce from the Far East to European markets. Simply place the question at one end of the task card, the answer at the other end, and cut the card in two in a jagged way (see Figure 12.1).

The same procedure applies to other questions and answers for that unit; you must make sure that each task card is cut in a unique jagged way. In doing this, you can ensure that only the correct questions and answers will fit together, because no

Figure 12.1

| The great African Rift Valley extends through which two continents and which countries? | Asia and Africa, from Syria, Israel, Jordan, Ethiopia, Kenya, Tanzania to Malawi and Mozambique |

other two pieces will fit together perfectly. You have created, in a manner of speaking, a special form of jigsaw puzzle, with cards mixed together, some bearing questions, others answers, and the object of the exercise is to bring order to the confusion, correctly fitting the proper answers to the questions on the first try. The tactual learner should enjoy playing with these pieces, fitting the correct questions and answers together time and again, and in the process learning crucial facts or concepts for a particular unit in a difficult academic area.

As time goes on, more elaborate task cards can be created in various units to help the learner remember new and difficult material. These may be of a size and shape so that they can be easily carried for use at times and in places where other materials might be inappropriate (see Figures 12.2 and 12.3).

Creating task cards such as these will increase the complexity of the exercise, and for tactual learners, the fun is figuring out the correct alignments, again on the first go. As the learner becomes more and more acquainted with this type of tactual exercise, the task cards can become more and more challenging and creative. The teacher must be the prime mover in this exercise and be the first to create the task cards in an area traditionally found difficult by many students. Once that is done, and once the students have understood what task cards are, the teacher will be able to assign the creation of new task cards in other areas of challenging learning to the tactual students themselves. In this way, tactual students will be utilizing their learning strength even more while learning new and difficult material. They may use their textbook or other source materials to create the task cards for a new unit and will thereby be learning it through their greatest learning strength.

If it is found that students are playing with the cards simply as jigsaw pieces and are looking only at the jagged edges and seeking to fit the correct pieces together simply on that basis, then the following approach is suggested. Construct the questions and answers in the usual way, but this time, on the reverse side, place a complete picture of some object—animal, vegetable, or mineral. Then, instead of

Figure 12.2

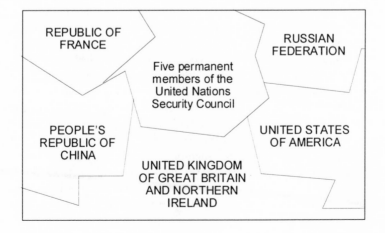

Figure 12.3

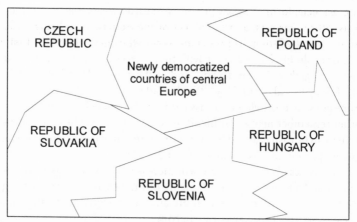

cutting the card into two pieces by means of a jagged edge, cut all the task cards vertically across, all identically. Now, the object of the exercise is to match the questions with the correct answers on the first attempt. Checking the answers is easy—by looking at the reverse of the two pieces. If, for example, the front end of a zebra is matched with the rear end of a dog, the answer is incorrect. If the pictures are taken from the new learning that the task cards are seeking to impart, there is reinforcement. So, for example, if the set of task cards is concerned with botany, then a series of pictures of the objects under examination on the reverse of the cards would be a good reinforcement.

FLIP CHUTE

Another tactual material is the flip chute. This is a simple stand-up tower, made from an empty half-gallon milk carton, which has two horizontal openings, one above the other on one of the four sides. Inside the tower, by means of two curved cards, a passageway, or flip chute, is created from the top opening to the bottom opening. A card with a question written on it is placed into the upper opening; it slides through the passageway, coming out of the bottom opening, bearing the correct answer to the question!

Again, nontactual learners will not consider this to be a legitimate method of learning anything, but it is not designed for them. The strongly tactual learner, for whom it *is* designed, will have a great deal of fun playing and, at the same time, learning from such a creation. It has been shown to be very effective for such learners, some of whom will play with it for hours on end.

Anecdotal stories abound about this device. One story, related by Dr. Kenneth Dunn, told him by a teacher-parent attending a learning-styles workshop several years ago, concerns a young grade school lad who was a good sportsman, even good in language skills at school, but who was not able to master his multiplication tables, despite every effort imaginable. His mother, knowing him to be the type of child who would not do what he was told to do, came across the idea of a flip chute from a friend whose child attended another school. "It worked for Timmy—why not for Bob?" she said to her friend.

The mother, aware of the routine behavior patterns of her son, created flip chute cards for the various multiplication tables like those in Figure 12.4. She made the flip chute herself and simply left it, with the cards, on the kitchen table, right next to the refrigerator, which was always the first stop her son made on arriving home from school. In he came, rushing into the kitchen, with his mother remaining quiet. "What's this?" he shouted, spotting the mysterious object on the table. "What's what?" his mother replied, coming into the kitchen. He was standing, refrigerator door not even opened, staring at the flip chute. "Oh. That's a magic mathematics machine," his mother replied. "Look," and she took a card from the pile which asked: "What is 7 x 7?" "Now, I place it in the top slot like this," she explained, as the card vanished into the top opening on the flip chute, "and out comes the answer like magic." The card said, "49."

Bob's eyes widened, as he looked in vain for electric wires—any wires—to explain this phenomenon. "I have something to do," his mother said, and she vanished. "Can I take this up to my room?" Bob asked. "OK," came the reply, and he vanished into his room. Television was forgotten, even dinner until he was summoned authoritatively, and the next morning he confessed he had been playing with the magic mathematics machine until two o'clock in the morning. His mother had made cards for all the multiplication tables, and he learned the lot with an enthusiasm unheard of until then. As Dr. Dunn tells it, this lad won the weekly math contest in class for the first time ever.

It may be platitudinous to say, but all students want to succeed; failure feels terrible, and if school represents failure, what students in their right mind will want to keep going there? If a simple tactual technique, such as the flip chute, allows strongly tactual learners to succeed in subjects where they have traditionally failed, then this is all to the good. Another thing should be clear: this type of technique works for tactual learners of all ages and ability levels. The questions on the cards will be commensurately more or less advanced, depending on the student, but the technique remains essentially the same.

Figure 12.4
Flip Chute Cards

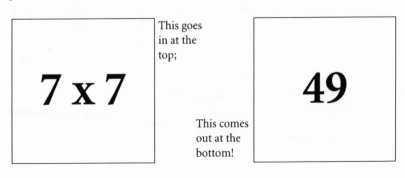

Again, teachers have to be the first to create this resource for their class, but once it is in place, then these very same students can be given an assignment to create similar materials in new areas of learning. Creative teachers and students will even find ways of building the milk carton into a shape which echoes the learning it is seeking to impart. Hence, the flip chute may be in the shape of a trash bin for a unit on recycling, or a tower computer for a unit on systems analysis. The possibilities are endless.

Here are the detailed instructions for making a flip chute like the one in Figure 12.5:

1. Carefully open the top of the carton without cutting anything.
2. Cut the corners of the lid down to the top of the carton.
3. Cut out the top opening of the flip chute:
   —— Measure down $1\frac{1}{2}$ inches from the top, and then $2\frac{1}{2}$ inches from the top.
   —— Draw lines across the width of the carton at these points.
   —— Cut out the 1-inch-wide rectangle made by the two lines.
4. Cut out the bottom opening of the flip chute:
   —— Measure up $1\frac{1}{2}$ inches from the bottom, and then $2\frac{1}{2}$ inches from the bottom.
   —— Draw lines across the width of the carton at these points.
   —— Cut out the 1-inch-wide rectangle made by the two lines.
5. Take a 5x8 index card and cut it so that it measures $6\frac{1}{2}$ inches by 3 inches.
6. Take a second 5x8 index card and cut it so that it measures $7\frac{1}{2}$ inches by 3 inches.
7. On the shorter, $6\frac{1}{2}$-inch strip, score and fold $\frac{1}{2}$-inch flaps at both ends, both folded in the same direction.
8. On the longer strip, score and fold a $\frac{1}{2}$-inch flap only at one end of the card.
9. Take the smaller strip and place it inside the carton. Hold it so that the two folded ends protrude through the openings, with the flaps pointing toward each other. Fold the lower flap over the upper edge of the bottom opening and then fold the upper flap over the bottom edge of the upper opening.
10. Use masking tape to secure the flaps into position. Make sure that the edge of the masking tape does not obstruct the openings into and out of the carton.
11. Insert the longer strip into the carton, with the folded edge first, and place the folded end over the bottom edge of the lower opening, with the fold facing downward.

Figure 12.5
The Flip Chute

$6\frac{1}{2}$ x $3\frac{1}{2}$ card
forming the inner
side of the chute.

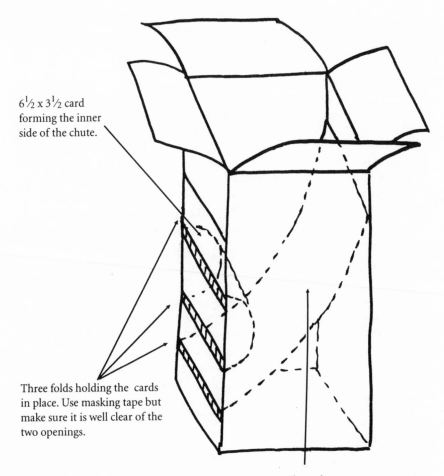

Three folds holding the cards
in place. Use masking tape but
make sure it is well clear of the
two openings.

$7\frac{1}{2}$ x $3\frac{1}{2}$ card attached at the
back—adjust the angle before
fixing by sliding a card through
before hand.

12. Use masking tape to secure the flaps into position. Make sure that the edge of the masking tape does not obstruct the opening out of the carton.

13. Cut a 3x5 index card into two pieces. Write a question on one side, turn it upside down and turn it over, and write the answer on the other side.

14. Hold the upper end of the longer strip inside the carton so that a passageway is created between the two strips from the top opening to the bottom. Insert the question/answer card into the top opening and see if it moves smoothly through the passageway to the bottom opening. If it does, then use masking tape to fix the top end of the longer strip to the back side of the carton. If it does not move smoothly from the top to the bottom opening, then adjust the strip a little up or down, as required. When the card moves swiftly and smoothly from the top opening to the bottom opening, use masking tape to secure the long strip into position against the back side of the carton.

15. Before sealing the top of the flip chute, make sure that there are no exposed masking tape edges which would impede the passage of the cards from the top to the bottom openings.

16. Fold the top of the flip chute with the four flaps, and seal with masking tape.

17. Apply contact paper of your own pattern to all surfaces of the flip chute to make it stronger. Again, make sure no edges impede the movement of the flip chute cards as they travel from the top opening to the bottom opening.

18. The card should enter the top opening with the question on top; when the answer emerges at the bottom, it should be the right way up. This means that the answer has to be put on the back of the card upside down.

THE PIC-A-HOLE

Another tactual technique is the pic-a-hole, sometimes called a poke-a-dot. This is simply a cardboard pocket containing large index cards, each containing a question in the unit under study (see Figure 12.6). There are three alternative answers offered along the bottom, in a kind of multiple choice format. Beneath each of the answers is a hole through the cardboard pocket. The student, using a golf tee or a similar small, round object, selects what he or she thinks is the correct answer. The tee is placed in the hole corresponding to the student's first choice, and if this is correct, the card will slip out of the pocket. If not, it will stay put and refuse to come out. This is simply because underneath the hole corresponding to the correct answer, a slot is cut out from the hole to the base of the index card, allowing the card to come out of the pocket. The slot, however, is invisible to the user.

Again, this simple little device is a delight to tactual learners, who might even create the cards themselves in order to become familiar with an area of great

Figure 12.6
The Pic-A-Hole

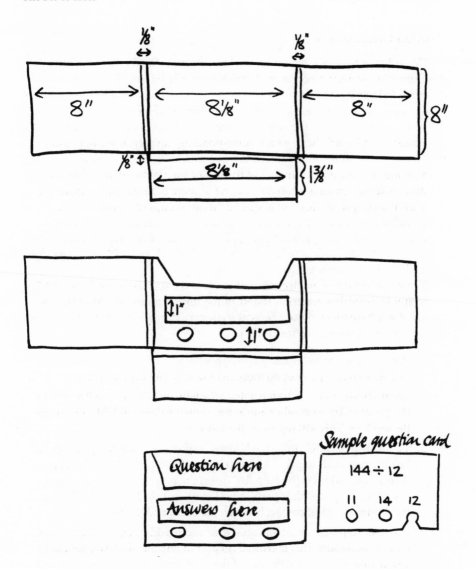

Fold one large flap back, then the smaller flap, then the second large flap. Punch the three holes, then use these to draw holes on the folds; then punch holes in them also.

challenge. Indeed, all these techniques should be reserved for those subjects and topics which present the greatest difficulty for learning in the student.

THE ELECTROBOARD

One other tactual resource, which might be the most fun for most students, even the nontactual learner, relies on an electrical circuit being completed and a battery-powered light going on as a consequence. Again, questions are asked in an area of challenge to the student, and a selection of answers is offered.

In the easiest format, the questions are ranked along the lefthand side of a rectangular cardboard sheet, with a corresponding number of answers along the right, not in the same order. Hence the question at the top of the list does not correspond to the answer standing at the top of the righthand list. One end of a continuity tester, which is a tool to discover if there is an electrical circuit that is intact, is placed against a brass brad next to the question, and the other end is placed on a brad next to the possible answer. If the answer is correct, the continuity tester, which carries a AA battery, will light up. If not, it stays dark. This, then, is simply another way for the student to have immediate feedback and, with the magic light, immediate reinforcement.

The construction of an electroboard, such as the one shown in Figure 12.7, is very simple, requiring materials found in the house: tinfoil, masking tape, brass brads (if you have them; if not, the local stationery store will have them), and clear contact paper, to strengthen the cardboard.

1. Punch a series of holes along two opposite sides of a piece of cardboard. As a first exercise, do not do more than four or five on each side.

2. Insert a brass brad into the top hole on the lefthand side. This will represent the question. Insert another into any hole on the righthand side other than the top hole. This will represent the answer.

3. Take a strip of tinfoil from the kitchen, making sure it is long enough to link the two brads together. Cut a strip about two inches thick. Fold once, then again, and press the strip flat. Insert the points of the brads into the end of the strip, and then press them flat against the foil. This will ensure maximum electrical contact between the brads and the foil.

4. Cover all exposed metal surfaces with the masking tape, using several strips if necessary. This is critical: no part of any metal surface should be visible to you at all, even the tips of the brad flaps. This completes the first question/answer circuit.

5. Do the same with question two, again carefully covering all exposed metal areas with the masking tape.

6. Use the continuity tester to see if each circuit is completed. Place the clip end of the tester against the question brad, and the pointed end of the test against the correct answer brad. If the circuit has been constructed correctly, the light will go on. Try the pointed end against all the other brads

Figure 12.7
The Electroboard

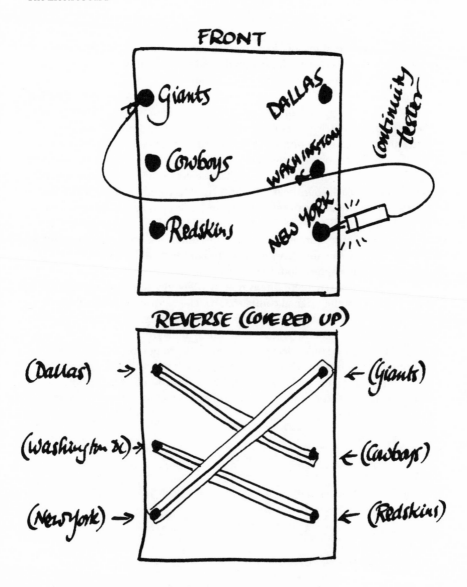

The correct answer is connected to the question by means of tin foil, which is then completely covered by masking tape to avoid any contact with the other connections.

to ensure that only the correct brad lights up. If the light goes on when the tester is pressed against another brad, then there is an incorrectly made circuit: the metal of one circuit is touching the metal of another circuit.

Perhaps one observation should be made here. Sometimes an electroboard will have a series of questions on the lefthand side, and the student is asked, for example, to say if they are correct or incorrect. That would mean that several circuits are linked to one brad, and the other questions to the other brad. In instances like this, circuits will be touching each other, but that is the intention of the maker.

Once the practitioner is used to this type of simple electroboard, other shapes and sizes are possible, depending on the information being conveyed. For example, a map of Europe electroboard may have the names of countries along the side, and a brad located in each unnamed country. The object of the exercise is to see if the student can name each country at the first turn. This could be a competitive game and, for a tactual student, very enjoyable as the learning is accomplished.

In the example in Figure 12.8, it will be seen that the correct response to the first statement is response number three (Queen Anne of Cleves was reputedly so unattractive that the English gave her this unflattering title). Statement three, on the other hand, has response four as the correct answer. Now, if the electroboard is turned upside down, statement one is now answered by response two, instead of response three as in the original configuration. The reader is advised at this point to ponder the figure carefully to understand this reasoning.

This means that a generic electroboard, which allows for Velcro-attached question sheets to be placed on it, clear of the brads, has two potential circuits, not one. But the board must be shaped asymmetrically so that there is no danger of placing the question sheets on the electroboard the wrong way round. The question/answer sheets will echo the shape of the electroboard and therefore can only be placed on it the correct way up.

Figure 12.8

• 1. Name the wife of King Henry VIII called the "Flanders Mare."	Elizabeth Tudor	•
• 2. Name the daughter of Queen Anne Boleyn.	Jane Grey	•
• 3. Whose daughter was "Bloody Mary"?	Anne of Cleves	•
• 4. Who was the "Nine Days Queen"?	Catherine of Aragon	•

This tactual material, of course, can also be made in the same shape as the Programmed Learning Sequence which deals with the same learning unit. In this way the student can relate all the material together, though it was learned in different ways.

CONCLUSION

These techniques, then, allow the learner to use his or her hands in mastering new and difficult learning at any level. The information is identical to that in the textbook, from which all the content for the questions has been drawn. The learner might actually enjoy these tactual exercises as he or she learns, and this might be a novel experience for some students! Additionally, these techniques may be used to reinforce previously learned material for those students whose primary learning preferences are other than tactual. For instance, visual students, who have read about new and difficult learning, might well employ these techniques to check themselves in that new knowledge and see if they can answer the questions correctly in the other, tactual format. Indeed, taking this a step further, any student could be asked to create task cards, flip chute cards, or pic-a-hole cards as a creative exercise and thereby deepen the new knowledge even further. This would be especially challenging in the case of the pic-a-hole, which usually depends on two plausible, but incorrect, responses in addition to the correct answer.

Some students demonstrate a strongly tactual ability to learn new and difficult material. This means that they use their hands to inform themselves of new understanding. The challenge for the teacher is to try and match learning materials with such a way of learning. Several suggested techniques which rely on manipulation have been presented in this chapter, and they can be vehicles for new and difficult information to learners. Teachers have to create a first set of these materials for students to use, but it will be excellent pedagogical practice to have such tactual students create their own tactual materials following their classroom introduction to this way of learning. They can be asked to translate the material in their textbooks into a question sheet for an electroboard or a set of task cards, for example, and this can be their means of learning more difficult material.

Over the years, students' tactual materials will accumulate, highlighting the difficult topics in various units in course work. For the maladroit teacher who does not do well putting tactual materials together, this can be a way of collecting the best materials made by the students (if they are prepared to let the teacher have them!). Either way, for some students, such techniques might well mean the difference between passing or failing, or scraping by as opposed to getting a good grade.

The conscientious teacher will indeed want to make sure every avenue has been taken which will allow students to succeed and grow. Identifying the learning style of students, therefore, is an obligation which cannot be stressed too much. Strongly tactual learners can be recognized and their needs accommodated by these techniques. Remember, however, that these same techniques are an excellent means of learning reinforcement for students who are not tactual learners, just as the ways in which new and difficult material is learned by them become reinforcement techniques for tactual learners in their turn. Therefore, the materials which begin to accumulate in classrooms can be used potentially by all students in the class, especially when they understand the ideas behind diverse ways of learning.

Challenging the best students to create new materials will be a third level of learning, because the students are being asked to do something new with their freshly assimilated material. Being able to do this successfully will truly demonstrate that the material has been properly mastered and can actually be utilized in new ways. In itself, this is an excellent pedagogical tool.

Hence there seems to be nothing but a winning learning condition here, one that is exciting for the teachers and students both. If students, by these means, have understood what had been traditionally the greatest teaching challenge of the year, then the teaching/learning process is alive and well and working as it should.

13

Using Kinesthetic Instructional Resources: Get on Your Feet and Step Forward!

Diane Mitchell and Eileen D'Anna

They file into the cafeteria one by one and look as if they would prefer to go to the dentist rather than sit through the session you are about to present. One teacher selects a seat at a table by himself and begins to grade papers. Another diligently works on her latest needlepoint project while the principal stands in the back of the cafeteria checking his watch. He informed you earlier that contractually the session must end by 3:30. You attempt to gather the group together to begin. Many remain by the refreshments, chatting. Don't they know that you are about to enlighten them about the latest methods in (fill in whatever trend is current)?

This group will surely be surprised when you flip on some music and shout, "Get on your feet!" Some people need to learn by moving, and by providing professional development that addresses this need, a presenter can be more effective than ever before.

WHAT KINESTHETIC INSTRUCTIONAL RESOURCES ARE

Staff development activities that are kinesthetic require whole-body movement, getting participants involved, and keeping them engaged during the workshop. This increased involvement leads to greater understanding and implementation of the newly presented practices once the teacher returns to the classroom. Besides being fun and motivating, these activities are an essential way to present new and difficult information to adults whose primary perceptual preference is kinesthetic. Once teachers have experienced this approach, they are likely to provide whole-body and real-life learning strategies to kinesthetic learners.

Educators are well aware that many children have a strong need for mobility, but that trait often is overlooked in adults. Perceptual preferences are biologically determined. Therefore, individuals have only minimal control over their learning-style preferences (Theis, 1979; Restak, 1979; Schmeck & Lockhard, 1983). Further-more, the learning style of adults tends to be consistent over time and for similar tasks (Elliot, 1975). Ingham (1991) demonstrated the importance of addressing the perceptual preference of adults during staff development. In a study conducted with the employees of a major bakery corporation, it was revealed that the majority of employees tested had combined tactual/kinesthetic perceptual preferences. When training methods matched their preferences, employees scored higher on follow-up tasks and reported a more positive attitude than when training was incompatible with their perceptual preferences. This research underscores the importance of recognizing an individual's need for activity-oriented instruction.

WHEN AND HOW TO USE KINESTHETIC INSTRUCTIONAL RESOURCES WITH ADULTS

There are many different ways that staff developers can incorporate kinesthetic activities into their workshops. If there are separate instructional centers in the workshop area, participants can move from station to station. Staff developers can also use a variety of whole-body games and activities. One of the most important qualities a staff developer can add to a presentation is creativity. Kinesthetic activities allow presenters to maximize their creative abilities. Consider adapting activities that work well with students in a classroom, such as dramatization, experimentation, and interviewing.

SAMPLES OF KINESTHETIC RESOURCES

The following kinesthetic resources and activities can be used by professional developers with adults. Once initiated, most adults will join in creating innovative kinesthetic learning experiences.

Floor and Wall Games

Floor and wall games are quick and inexpensive to make and can be used in a variety of ways. They are easily transported by the staff developer and can be used over and over again. To design a floor game, the following materials are needed: a shower curtain liner, a permanent magic marker, rolls of colored plastic tape, index cards, envelopes, Velcro strips, tossing objects such as a bean bag, dice, spinners, and, of course, your imagination! Choose a board or game design that is appropriate for conveying the information being presented in the workshop. Figures 13.1, 13.2, and 13.3 are examples of different game ideas. Using the markers, draw the game design right onto the shower curtain. Include instructions for playing the game. Questions and answers can be written onto index cards. Adhere all game pieces and game questions and answers with Velcro to the curtain or in envelopes used as storage. The game boards can be laid on the floor or hung onto the wall. For wall games, large poster board or oak tag can be substituted for the shower curtain.

Tic-Tac-Toe Game. To make this game (see Figure 13.1), draw or use plastic colored tape to form the nine boxes of the tic-tac-toe boxes of the poster board. Make 5-inch squares of oak tag with large Xs and Os on them. Put them into envelopes and attach the envelopes to the game board. Find or design pockets to hold questions and attach them to each tic-tac-toe square. Fill each pocket with four to six questions written on 3x5 index cards. Put the questions on one side and the answers on the other. Two participants play at a time. The one with an X chooses a square to attempt. The other player selects the first question from the pocket in that box and reads it to him or her. If the question is answered correctly, an X is put into that square. If the question is answered incorrectly, no X is added. The person with the O then has a turn. Play continues until one player has tic-tac-toe.

Redesign a Classroom. This game can be used in conjunction with a workshop on accommodating the environmental and sociological learning-style needs of students. A game board is designed to look like an empty classroom (see Figure 13.2). The participants arrange the game pieces (classroom furniture) to redesign a classroom.

Match the Learning-Style Element with the Appropriate Stimulus. In this game, 3x5 cards containing the 21 elements of the Dunn and Dunn Learning Styles Model are placed into an envelope. Participants select one element and place it next to the appropriate stimulus (see Figure 13.3). Correct answers are written on the back of the cards. (*Variation*: Each participant tosses a beanbag onto one of the stimulus strands. Then he or she has ten seconds to walk quickly to the cards spread out on a table and return to place it in the correct space.)

Figure 13.1
Tic-Tac-Toe Game

Tic-Tac-Toe

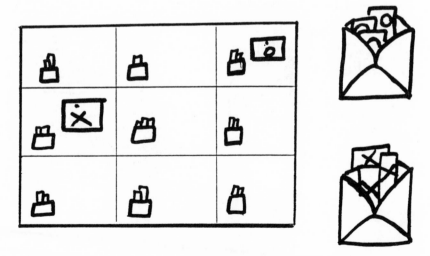

Directions: Select a square and pick a question. Mark an X or an O if the question is answered correctly.

Figure 13.2
Room Design

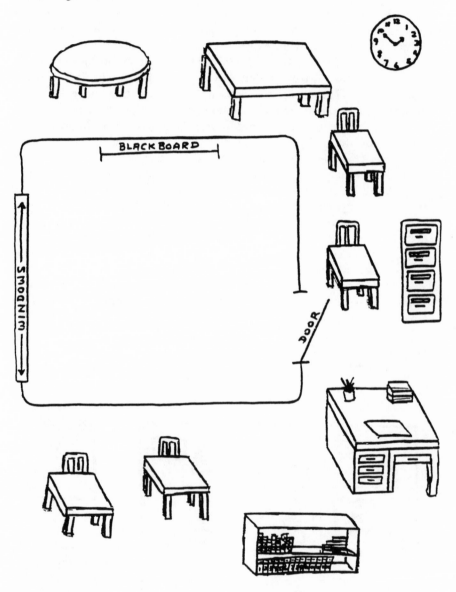

Figure 13.3
Matching the Learning-Style Element with the Appropriate Stimulus

Element Match-Up

```
┌─────────────────────────────────────────────────────────┐
│   Environmental                                           │
├───────────────────────────────────────────────────────────┤
│   Emotional                                               │
├───────────────────────────────────────────────────────────┤
│   Sociological                                            │
├───────────────────────────────────────────────────────────┤
│   Physiological                                           │
├───────────────────────────────────────────────────────────┤
│   Psychological                                           │
├───────────────────────────────────────────────────────────┘
│                                                           │
└───────────────────────────────────────────────────────────┘
```

Directions: Select a card from the envelope. Look at the element and place it in the space next to the appropriate stimulus.

Role-Playing

Role-playing activities offer staff developers an opportunity to actively involve participants in the workshop as they learn and develop new skills. Participants can function as teachers and students in a mock classroom. Teachers will have a ball playing the role of their students and will learn from the experience as well. (*Variation:* Briefly describe on 3x5 cards different kinds of learning from the Dunn and Dunn Learning Styles Model and different kinds of teachers based on the Dunn and Dunn Teaching Styles Inventory. Have each participant act out his or her role based on the cards.)

Pantomime

Pantomime is an effective and easy way to introduce a topic or to review one quickly. Participants act out the skill being taught. For example, when introducing the 21 elements of the Dunn and Dunn model, have participants act out each element. Once they have acted it out, they will never forget it! You can just imagine the laughter that will abound as participants try and guess the elements as their colleagues perform them.

Progression

Progression is an excellent strategy to use when teaching a new skill or process that involves multiple steps. As the participants say and do each one of the steps in a newly learned process, they take one step forward. The step of the learning process is associated with the physical area on the floor. The bodily movement involved in the activity helps kinesthetic learners learn a sequential process. (*Variation:* Number the steps and place question cards next to each one. Have the participants throw a die and proceed to walk the number of steps thrown on the die and answer the questions next to each step. This can be self-scoring or used as a game with teams and point scores.)

Associated Action

This technique works on a principle similar to progression. When a participant answers a question, he or she stands in a designated space. That space then becomes associated with the answer. A kinesthetic learner will often be able to recall that information in the future by visualizing the physical area in which the question was answered. Graphics and other visuals should be added for global learners, and words and numbers for analytics.

SUMMARY

The whole-body movement during the learning process is what helps a kinesthetic learner learn new and difficult information. It is a prerequisite for many learners. For the participants whose primary perceptual strength is not kinesthetic, whole-body activities can be fun and can serve as an engaging and interesting reinforcement.

Extensive research has been done in the area of perceptual preferences and learning style (Dunn, Bauer, Gemake, Gregory, Primavera, & Signer, 1994; Ingham, 1991; Kroon, 1985; Martini, 1986; Buell & Buell, 1987). Research concerning adults who learn kinesthetically is still relatively new and therefore limited compared to that for the other perceptual modalities. Perhaps this is the reason why most professional developers overlook this critical need. Nevertheless, the research is conclusive and noteworthy. Therefore, staff developers who want to be effective with all participants would be wise to incorporate kinesthetic activities and resources into their presentations.

REFERENCES

Buell, B. G., & Buell, N. A. (1987). Perceptual modality preferences as a variable in the effectiveness of continuing education for professionals (Doctoral dissertation, University of Southern California, 1987). *Dissertation Abstracts International, 48,* 283A.

Dunn, R., Bauer, E., Gemake, J., Gregory, J., Primavera, L., & Signer, B. (1994). Matching and mismatching junior high school learning disabled and emotionally handicapped students' perceptual preferences on mathematics scores. *Teacher Education Journal, 5*(1), 3–14.

Elliot, P. H. (1975). An exploratory study of adult learning styles. Unpublished research report (ERIC Document Reproduction Service No. ED 116016).

Ingham, J. (1991). Matching instruction with employee perceptual preferences significantly increases training effectiveness. *Human Resource Development Quarterly, 2*(1), 53–64.

Kroon, D. (1985). An experimental investigation of the effects on the academic achievement and the resultant administrative implications of instruction congruent and incongruent with secondary, industrial arts students' learning style perceptual preferences (Doctoral dissertation, St. John's University, 1985). *Dissertation Abstracts International, 46,* 3247A.

Martini, M. (1986). An analysis of the relationships between and among computer-assisted instruction, learning style perceptual preferences, attitudes, and the science achievement of seventh grade students in a suburban, New York school district (Doctoral dissertation, St. John's University, 1986). *Dissertation Abstracts International, 47,* 877A.

Restak, R. (1979). *The brain: The last frontier.* New York: Doubleday.

Schmeck, R., & Lockhard, F. (1983). Development of a self-report inventory for assessing individual differences in learning processes. *Applied Psychological Measurement, 1,* 413–431.

Theis, A. P. (1979). A brain-behavior analysis of learning style. In J. W. Keefe (Ed.), *Student learning styles: Diagnosing and prescribing programs* (pp. 55–61). Reston, VA: National Association of Secondary School Principals.

14

Using a Multisensory Instructional Package: A Sense-ational Approach

Marjorie S. Schiering and Rita Glaser Taylor

"It was early June, and . . . "

"No, it was the end of May," said Janet.

"Okay, whatever."

Anyway, we were sitting in Dr. Rita Dunn's learning-styles class, and Dr. Kenneth Dunn was helping us construct tactile materials for the Multisensory Instructional Package (MIP), when Janet was heard to say, "I can't do this." "Do what?" asked Ann.

"I can't make these things. Just give me a book and let me read about it," countered Janet.

"I love working with my hands. I'll make yours *and* mine!" "Okay! When?" she queried.

"Why don't we get together over the weekend and we'll work on the materials," answered Ann.

"Great! My house, Sunday afternoon."

Sunday morning found Janet telling her two teenage children that they would have to keep the stereo off Sunday afternoon so that she and her classmate Ann could work. Ann arrived 30 minutes late, laden with what looked like bags of food. "Hi!" welcomed Janet.

"I've got the carrots and popcorn. Where's the living room? Gee, it's kind of quiet here! I thought you had teenagers—where's the loud music? Is everyone gone? This place is too quiet, but lovely!" Ann commented. Janet took a deep breath before responding. "I need quiet! The living room is out of the question as a work area, and any food would surely be a distraction," she said as she turned up the lights.

Ann realized that she and Janet were at opposite ends of the learning-styles spectrum. With her preferences, she obviously was a global processor, whereas Janet was certainly an analytic (big time!).

"All right, Ann, tell me again what we have to make for the Multisensory Instructional Package."

"Well, it contains instructions (both written and on audiotape); a Programmed Learning Sequence (with an accompanying audiotape for auditory learners and nonreaders and a videotape for visual learners); a Contract Activity Package (for nonconforming students and those who like choices); tactual and kinesthetic materials which include a flip chute, pic-a-hole, learning wheel, electroboard, task cards, and a floor game; and finally, a test."

"Now I understand! The Multisensory Instructional Package is for students who like structure. For them, it offers the Programmed Learning Sequence or PLS. The MIP meets the needs of a cross-section of learners. It is good for those classified as learning disabled who need more direct intervention, for average students, and for advanced students who can progress at their own rate. It's also for slow learners who require more time to grasp new material. Furthermore, during periods of independent study, an interested youngster can go to an MIP and learn about a topic for the simple pleasure of learning, not merely because I assigned it! Most important, every part of the MIP is self-correcting. The students get immediate feedback about their responses," responded Janet.

"I like the MIP because the Programmed Learning Sequence, audio and visual tapes, and tactual/kinesthetic materials can be used repeatedly," Ann added. "Each instructional package focuses on a single objective or concept to be taught. There's something for everyone because there are visual, auditory, tactual, and kinesthetic activities."

"It is valuable because students can work alone on one part of the package. Those who enjoy working in small groups or with a peer can do that too," bubbled Janet.

"What I really like is that global learners like me can take the MIP anywhere, so that we can sit comfortably, spread out, and even snack while working. Such an individual can put on a set of headphones and listen to music. Most important, individuals can choose the materials according to their perceptual strengths," reflected Ann. "It appeals to students who need to move around while learning and who find it difficult to sit while listening to a teacher."

"So, for students who like to take breaks whenever they wish and continue their work at their own pace, the MIP is effective. However, if the student needs direct interaction with teachers or other authority figures, the Multisensory Instructional Package may not be suitable," replied Janet.

"Students can choose the activities they find most beneficial, especially if they're already familiar with the topic," noted Ann.

"That's right! Some of my students had studied pollution last year with Mr. DeJulia, so they needed only to go over the most appropriate materials for them. For instance, Robert, a kinesthetic learner, reviewed with the floor game," shared Janet.

"In a nutshell, the MIP is an asset to teachers who want to individualize their classrooms by addressing students' learning styles, but are inhibited by class size, time constraints, and heterogeneous grouping," Ann summarized.

THE FLIP CHUTE

Figures 14.1 through 14.7 depict the various steps, described below, of constructing a flip chute.

Materials

One empty half-gallon milk container
Ruler
Pencil
Scissors
Two (2) 5x8 index cards (Dunn & Dunn, 1992)

1. Open the top of the empty half-gallon milk container.
2. Cut the side folds of the top portion down to the top of the container.
3. Place a ruler horizontally across the top edge of one side of the container and draw a line along the bottom edge of the ruler.
4. Place the top of the ruler along the drawn line and draw a line along the bottom edge of the ruler again.
5. Cut out this rectangular space.
6. Place the ruler horizontally along the bottom of the container and draw a line along the top of the ruler. Place the bottom of the ruler along the drawing and draw a line along the top edge. Cut out this rectangular space.
7. Take out two (2) 5x8 index cards. Cut one so that it measures $7\frac{1}{2}$" by $3\frac{1}{2}$". Cut the other to measure $6\frac{1}{2}$" by $3\frac{1}{2}$".

Figure 14.1

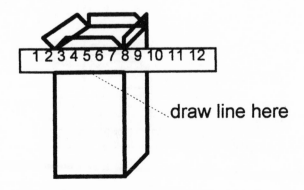

Created by M. Schiering and R. Taylor. Redesigned by K. Burke.

8. Fold down ½" at both ends of the smaller strip. Fold down ½" at one end of the longer strip.

9. Take the longer strip and place it inside the container with the folded end facing downward, over the bottom edge of the bottom opening. Tape this securely to the outside of the container. Tape the other end to the top part of the inside of the container so that there is a slight slope in the index card strip.

10. Form a backward "C" by placing the smaller strip in the palm of your hand. Place this inside the container so that the folded portions face downward and upward respectively on the outside of the upper and lower slots of the container. Secure to the outside of the container with tape.

11. To make the instructional cards for the flip chute, cut pieces that are 2" by 2½" in size. On one side of the card write the question, with the answer upside down on the flip side.

12. Insert the question card with the question upright into the top slot of the flip chute. Let it slide down. Voila! The answer magically appears!

13. Decorate according to the theme of the MIP.

Figure 14.2

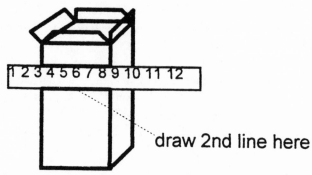

Created by K. Burke. Redesigned by M. Schiering and R. Taylor based on Dunn and Dunn (1992).

Figure 14.3

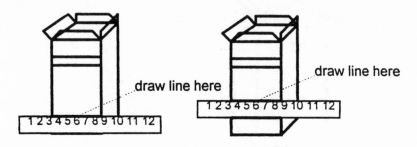

Created by M. Schiering and R. Taylor. Redesigned by K. Burke.

Figure 14.4

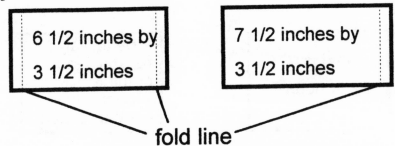

fold line

Created by M. Schiering and R. Taylor. Redesigned by K. Burke based on Dunn and Dunn (1992).

Figure 14.5

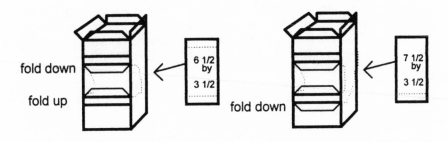

Created by M. Schiering and R. Taylor. Redesigned by K. Burke based on Dunn and Dunn (1992).

Figure 14.6

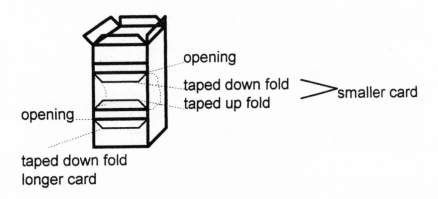

Created by M. Schiering and R. Taylor. Redesigned by K. Burke based on Dunn and Dunn (1992).

Figure 14.7

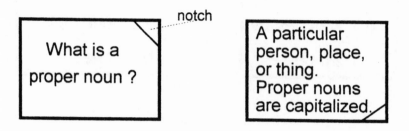

Created by M. Schiering and R. Taylor. Redesigned by K. Burke based on Dunn and Dunn (1992).

THE PIC-A-HOLE

A pic-a-hole is more of an introductory than a reinforcement type of resource. It offers choices from among three options, should a youngster's first or even second choice be incorrect. Its self-correcting feature ensures eventual success in a private, nonthreatening environment (Dunn & Dunn, 1992). Figure 14.8 depicts a tracing for the pic-a-hole.

Figure 14.8
The Pic-A-Hole

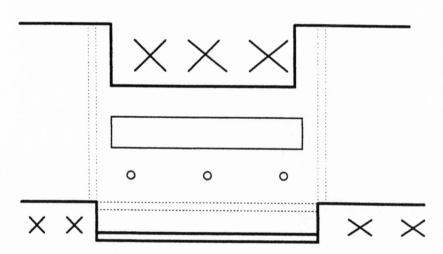

XX = open area
o = hole punch area
.... = scored area

THE ELECTROBOARD

All the tactile resources should have the same shape, and that shape should reflect the theme (Dunn & Dunn, 1992). Figure 14.9 shows an electroboard.

Materials

Poster board
Colored markers
Aluminum foil
$\frac{3}{4}$" or 1" masking tape
Continuity tester
Scissors

1. Begin with two pieces of poster board of exactly the same size and shape.

2. Section the left side of the electroboard to correspond to the number of questions you will be asking. Section the right side similarly for the answers.

3. Using the hole punch, make one hole at the point where each question will appear on the left side of the poster board. Corresponding holes should be placed where the answers will appear.

4. Print the questions and answers on the poster board next to the punched holes. Answers should not be directly across from the questions.

5. Turn the poster board over. Place a $\frac{1}{4}$"-wide strip of aluminum foil in a line, connecting a question with the correct answer. The foil should begin at the hole for the question and end at the hole for the answer. Cover the foil strip with $\frac{3}{4}$" to 1" masking tape so that there is no foil exposed.

6. Using a continuity tester, purchased in a hardware or automotive store, check the circuit.

Figure 14.9

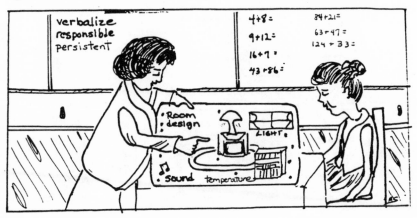

7. Repeat steps 5 and 6 with the remaining questions and answers. Make sure no foil strip touches another foil strip.

8. Cover the circuitry with the second piece of poster board. Tape the perimeter of both cards together, or use double-faced tape.

TASK CARDS

Task cards respond to a youngster's need to see and touch at the same time (see Figure 14.10). They are effective for tactual students at all levels (Dunn & Dunn, 1992).

Materials

Colored oaktag or cardboard
Colored markers
Scissors

1. Cut colored oaktag or cardboard into desired shape.

2. On the left side of each shape, write the vocabulary word or question related to your topic. On the right side place the definition or answer to the question.

3. Either laminate or cover each shape with clear contact paper to protect and keep it clean for repeated use.

4. Cut each shape in half, using a different pattern each time (e.g., zigzag cut, straight line, off center, or diagonal).

5. Package the set of cards in a box and place a title on the top that describes the task cards inside.

Figure 14.10

Model of a Task Card Holder

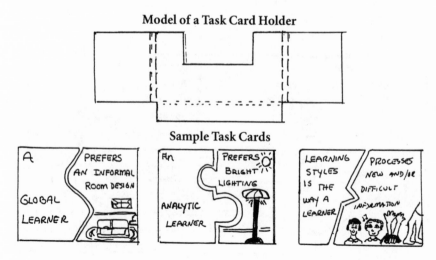

Sample Task Cards

KINESTHETIC FLOOR GAMES

Floor Games are particularly good for kinesthetic learners, who don't respond to direct verbal instruction, lectures, "chalk talks," and textbook assignments. A kinesthetic learner is one who learns through whole body involvement. Instruction should be introduced through an individual's strongest perceptual strength (Dunn & Dunn, 1992). One floor game is illustrated in Figure 14.11.

Materials

Opaque shower curtain liner
Permanent markers or acrylic paint
Index cards
Felt tip pen

1. Decide on the topic of your MIP.
2. Draw a design with the marker or paint related to the topic you've chosen.
3. Write questions on the index cards related to the topic. Write the answers on the back of the index card.
4. These questions should direct the learner to move to different places on the game board upon successfully answering the questions.
5. Write the directions for playing the game on the shower curtain liner or on an index card.

Variations include having the learner hop, skip, jump, dance, and so on, from playing space to playing space, from question to question, and having him or her move sequentially from start to finish by answering a question at each playing space.

Figure 14.11

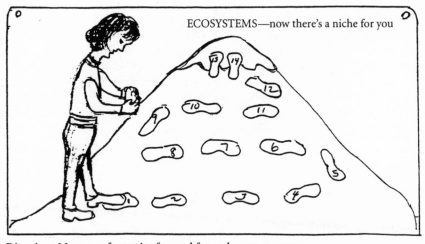

Directions: Move one foot print forward for each correct answer.

THE PROGRAMMED LEARNING SEQUENCE

The Programmed Learning Sequence or PLS should be designed in the shape of the theme of the unit being presented. It is highly structured in its format (Dunn & Dunn, 1992).

Materials

10 to 20 5x8 index cards
Two snap-on rings
Hole puncher
Colored pens
Laminate

1. Begin with a global or humorous story or cartoon.
2. All pages should be numbered with the words Frame #1, Frame #2, and so on, at the top.
3. Present material in small, sequential "chunks." Each frame should build upon the one immediately preceding it.
4. Each frame should end with an item that requires an answer in either a completion or multiple-choice format.
5. On the back of each frame supply the correct answer.
6. Include mini-review tactile activities every four (4) to seven (7) frames for reinforcement of the information.
7. Place a front and back cover on the PLS and laminate each page.
8. Supply a grease pencil so the learner can write in and wipe off his or her answers.

THE CONTRACT ACTIVITY PACKAGE

The Contract Activity Package (CAP) permits individual pacing so that average, above average, gifted, and/or nonconforming students may learn as quickly or as slowly as they are able to master the material. These can be designed so students can work on their current academic level but master concepts or facts through resources that explain the content in a way that is comfortable for that learner. Because the student works on the CAP by himself or herself, he or she becomes personally responsible for what is required; thus the CAP promotes independence. Youngsters are permitted to learn in ways they find most comfortable (Dunn & Dunn, 1992).

The elements of a Contract Activity Package are as follows:

1. *Objectives* describe the skills or information that the student is responsible for learning.

2. *Resource alternatives* allow the student to use a variety of resources: books, films, transparencies, interviews, visits.

3. *Small group techniques* offer peer interaction for learning the material, such as brainstorming, role-playing, and team learning.

4. *Activity alternatives* require the student to use the newly learned information in a creative way, such as drawings, songs, presentations, and poetry.

5. *Reporting alternatives* provide opportunities for the student to share what he has learned with classmates.

6. *Assessment:* A test of the material is given before exposure so that a student is able to skip over the objectives he or she has already mastered. In addition, a test is given at the conclusion so that the student can verify what he or she has learned.

It is through the objectives that the student gets an overview of what will be covered. Activity alternatives require the student to use the newly learned information, particularly in a creative way. Research shows that individuals retain more when information is used creatively.

THE MULTISENSORY INSTRUCTIONAL PACKAGE FACILITATES LEARNING IN STYLE

Each package focuses on a single unit, concept, or theme within the subject area or curriculum. For example, an MIP can teach about plants—the parts of a plant, how they reproduce, what they need to grow; or ecosystems—the various types (underwater, forest, desert) and habitats and niches. Whatever the theme of the MIP, it is clear to students what they will learn as a result of working with the package because of the goals listed on the first page of the Programmed Learning Sequence. The cover and two titles (global and analytic) make the topic clear to everyone!

Written and audiotaped directions guide the student through the package, offering alternative routes to the same goals, depending on his or her prediagnosed learning style. Students are given the opportunity to experience the contents using all four senses—visual, auditory, tactual, and kinesthetic.

Feedback is immediate. All materials are self-correcting; students do not have to rely on anyone else to let them know how well they are doing. Mistakes are easily corrected. Through the use of tests and reporting and activity alternatives included in the MIP, students can demonstrate what they have learned.

Peer competition is reduced for those hampered by it because only the student and the teacher are aware of how well the student is doing. Slower learners can work at their own pace without comparison to others.

The individuality the Multisensory Instructional Package affords makes it appealing to some students at every learning level. This holds true for many kindergartners who need to run, jump, and skip in order to learn, and for adults who need to manipulate, piece together, or listen and relisten to an audiotape.

Multisensory Instructional Packages have been used successfully both in class-rooms with young learners and in staff development with adult learners (see sample adult materials in Dunn & Griggs, 1998).

REFERENCE

Dunn, R., & Dunn, K. (1992). *Teaching elementary students through their individual learning styles.* Boston: Allyn & Bacon, Inc.

Dunn, R., & Griggs, S. A. (Eds) (1998). *Learning styles and the nursing profession.* NY: National League of Nursing.

15

Epilogue:
Getting Started before It's Too Late

Ilisa D. Sulner

Principal Jones has allocated this year's precious instructional development funds on a series of workshops designed to improve instructional strategies in the classroom. Imagine, then, how he feels, upon entering the school auditorium, to find several teachers talking among themselves, one reading the newspaper, one correcting test papers, and one sound asleep. The speaker, a renowned speaker with a great deal to offer, is continuing his efforts to impart his wealth of knowledge but it is clearly a futile effort; the teachers have entered the no-fly zone.

REALITY STRIKES!

Principal Jones is only too aware of how poor some of the teaching is in the classrooms; he has a stack of unsatisfactory observations with which to support this theory. He also has falling student test scores, poor student and staff attendance, and increasing numbers of incident reports resulting from behavioral outbursts. The school is stuck in the muck and mire of mediocrity and is headed for disaster. Principal Jones must take action and realizes he must develop both a short- and a long-term approach to bring his school back. He needs a mission, and he needs to act fast.

Principal Jones, alias General Jones, must now engage in "chicken and egg" strategic thinking and planning because he wants desperately to decide which came first: the ineffectiveness of the instructional methods employed by his staff or the increasingly disturbing behaviors of his students. This cannot be determined—the answer is fraught with cyclical logic. General Jones knows he has a twofold problem on his hands. He ponders which to attack first, trying to decide the greatest threat to the success of his school and instructional program. Experience has taught that the hardest attack is head on, resulting in confrontation and ill will. It is as meaningless as awakening the sleeping teacher, and it will only increase feelings of frustration and malevolence. Experience also has taught that it is usually easier to go around the flank and trap the enemy from behind, leaving them nowhere to go but into guarded territory which may lead to surrender, but in the right place. Administrators instinctively know that once a teacher is in the learning zone and tastes the sweetness of successful teaching, there is no escape. The benevolent trap which can empower the learning and accomplishment is "learning styles," and Principal Jones must now devise a clever way to ease this concept and program direction into daily planning and implementation.

"CHALK AND TALK" IS NOT FOR EVERYBODY

There are endless tales of woe from administrators all over this country, of teacher burnout, of students out of control, of parents in despair, and ultimately of burgeoning numbers of youngsters entering the juvenile justice system. These issues are not mutually exclusive of one another and are in direct linkage with definitive cause and effect factors. Educators can argue why this is happening endlessly, but it really does not matter; we just have to put an end to it with a method that will empower teachers to teach and students to learn and, indeed, parents to parent. Therefore, instructional leaders are charged with establishing and maintaining pedagogical standards that are believed to have a direct linkage to student performance. These instructional leaders are well aware of the impact classroom programming has on student behavior, staff morale, and school spirit. Teachers, according to the manner in which they teach, have the power to engage and challenge students in a style compatible with their learning-style preference and cognitive ability. Dunn and Griggs (1989) reported on the "quiet revolution" in American secondary schools, indicating that in several schools across the United States, the implementation of learning styles not only had benefited the students, but had assisted the teachers to "come alive" and realize a renewed sense of "really helping" their students. Stone (1992) tells the tale of turning a school around, all due to the infusion of learning styles.

DON'T ASK WHY—JUST THROW THE STICK!

Teachers learn all too well what they are supposed to be teaching. A learned colleague of this author, Marilyn Stolper, of the Board of Education of the City of New York, charges teachers with figuring out the why: Why are you teaching that skill to that student? After answering that question, teachers must then determine how, where, and when they will teach the skill. The answer, again, lies in the determination of learning styles. The answer to these questions crosses all levels of ability or disability and reaches cognition at its most basic and advanced level. The classic flow of a lesson, from beginning (motivation) to middle (development) to end (culmination), may not work well with all learners. At times, some students respond and "awaken" if the lesson is initiated in midstream. This seems to pique curiosity and, again, seems to be related to learning-style theory. Teachers may need to restructure how information is presented to students based on their individual preferences and needs. The outcome at the conclusion of a lesson may not be as apparent or as measurable as an observer would desire.

Principal Jones realizes that caught up in the middle of this fracas is the looming issue of teacher observation. School administrators usually seek to observe the three sequential elements of the developmental lesson for the determination of teacher ratings. However, as with the failure of the classical format of staff development, there comes a realization that the standard method of observation does not improve instruction. Principal Jones can merely shake his head in amazement. Staff development has just become part of the observation process, which can be a learning process for teachers if conducted properly. Principal Jones realizes that the situation he has defined is truly complicated.

SIPS AND TIPS

How then to combine informal staff development with the observational process and the incorporation of learning styles for students and staff? Principal Jones now becomes Instructional Leader Jones. He begins by spreading the gospel. He conducts informal observations in each classroom and writes a reaction to each, accompanied by an article about learning styles and another about the curriculum area that was being taught. He makes sure to state the positive aspects of the lesson, he places no blame on the teacher for what he identifies as a weakness, and he provides suggestions, supported by research, to assist the teacher in achieving improved pedagogical skills. Instructional Leader Jones does his own homework and reacquaints himself with current trends, research, and best practices. He decides that the expertise for improvement lies within the staff, and he determines two methods for exploiting this potential: SIPS—Sharing Instructional Professional Strategies—and TIPS—Teachers Involved in Professional Sharing.

These methods become the buzzwords and the norm of school activity. Newsletters are developed to support sharing, staff meetings identify one teacher a week (on a voluntary basis) to present a success, and collaboration becomes the norm. Classroom and grade teams meet to determine how and when to implement instructional changes. Parties are held to honor the learning-style preference of the week; students and staff alike all determine their preferences and then decide how much of the day can be dedicated to this manner of instruction. Teachers are learning how to identify the teaching skills they possess as well as how to apply them to new situations, as demanded by the identification of student learning-style preferences. Teachers begin sharing their ideas, exemplary programs, and failures with one another. Teachers read and contribute to the school newsletter and begin to think how to apply what they have read to their students. They no longer feel powerless to change their teaching and begin to uplift the curriculum to a status heretofore unseen in this school.

Instructional Leader Jones continues on his mission to provide support and enthusiasm for achievement, both for staff and for students, and continues to revive professional spirits by disseminating research articles, conducting breakfast and lunch hour "strategic planning" sessions, and determining, by consensus, just how to spend next year's professional development budget. In fact, the teacher who slept during that first workshop is in charge of the committee for professional development. Principal Jones is not ruling by committee; he is leading by example. Principal Jones is encouraging and, in fact, demanding feedback and sharing. Principal Jones is empowering teachers to develop an awareness of what they are doing and why it is successful or not. Principal Jones is providing the content for team meetings. Principal Jones, alias General Jones, alias Instructional Leader Jones, looks toward the future with renewed interest and satisfaction for a process well conceived and implemented.

REFERENCES

Dunn, R., & Griggs, S. A. (1989). A quiet revolution: Learning styles and their application to secondary schools. *Holistic Education Review, 2*(4), 9–14.

Stone, P. (1992). How we turned around a problem school. *Principal, 71*(2), 34–36.

Index

role-playing, 127; room design for, 126; samples of, 124–128; tic-tac-toe, 125; what they are, 123–124; when and how to use, 124

Learning style(s): accommodating, 8; definition, 4; environmental preferences, 9; identifying adults' styles, 4–5; introduction to, 3–4; matching elements with stimuli, 127; Network, 36; responding to participants', 49–54; sociological preferences, 9; technology training, 42–46; time-of-day preferences, 10; tools, latest, 41; model, 7
Learning Styles Network, 36

Motivation, 12, 26; incentives for, 19, 27–28
Multisensory Instructional Package(s) (MIPs), 131–142; contract activity package(s), 140–141; effective, for whom, 132; electroboard, 137–138; facilitating learning, 141–142; flip chute, 133–136; kinesthetic floor games, 139; pic-a-hole, 136; programmed learning sequence(s), 140; task cards, 138

Needs assessment, 58

Perceptual preferences, implications of, 10
Persistence, 12
Personal Reinforcement Checklist, 28
Physiological elements, 6
Physiological preferences, responding to, 44–45, 53–54
Pic-a-hole, 116–118, 36
Planning, for staff development, 17–22
Processing styles, adults', 8; implications of, 8–9; responding to, 45
Productivity Environmental Preference Survey, 5; elements, 6, 50
Programmed Learning Sequence(s) (PLSs), 11, 79–86, 140; assessment, 84; effective, for whom, 81; 84–85; frames, 83–84; global introduction, 81; Multisensory Instructional Package,

140; reinforcement, 84–85; shape, 81–82; tactual components, 81–82
Psychological elements, 6

Responsibility (conformity vs. nonconformity), 12
Reporting alternatives, 88, 91, 94–95, 97, 101–102
Resources, for CAPs, 104–105; kinesthetic, 123–129; tactual, 109–122
Restlessness, implications of, 11

Small group techniques, 95–97, 103, 127
Sociological elements, 6
Sociological preferences, 5; implications of, 9–10; responding to, 44, 52–53
Staff development: assistance, 30; avoiding resistance to, 37–38, 67–68; baby steps, 12–14; composers of music for, 76; composing for, 77–78; Contract Activity Packages, using for, 87–107; conventional, 4; decision-making process for, 25; evaluation of, 65–70; improvement of, 73–78; incentives for, 27–29; informal forms of, 33–34; learning outside, 36; learning-style based, 4; motivation, 26; music, using for, 73–78; needs assessment, 58; new approaches, 35; new roles and structures, 35; planning for, 17–22; programmed learning sequences for, 79–86; reform process, 60–62; selection process for developers, 58–60; tactual resources, 109–122; up-grading skills for, 38
St. John's University, 5, 36
Strategies, sharing, 145–146
Structure, 12

Tactual: electroboard, 118–121, 137–138; flip chute, 112–116, 133–136; kinesthetic component of, 123–128; pic-a-hole, 116–118, 136; resources, 109–122; task cards, 110–112, 138
Task cards, 85, 110–112, 138
Team learning, 98–100; sample questions, 100

About the Editors and Contributors

DANIEL T. ARCIERI is an Instructional Support Technician and Adjunct Associate Professor, Department of Biological Sciences, State University of New York at Farmingdale. He is a candidate in St. John's University's Instructional Leadership Doctoral Program.

ERIC BRAND is a Hackensack, New Jersey, high school English teacher and a candidate in St. John's University's Instructional Leadership Doctoral Program.

SUSAN BRAND is a Nyack, New York, elementary school teacher and a candidate in St. John's University's Instructional Leadership Doctoral Program.

KAREN BURKE, Assistant Principal, St. Elizabeth Seton School, Diocese of New Brooklyn, is an Instructional Leadership doctoral candidate and a certified staff trainer for St. John's University's Center for the Study of Learning and Teaching Styles, New York.

ROGER CALLAN, Ed.D., a secondary school teacher and former principal, completed St. John's University's Instructional Leadership Doctoral Program as a certified staff trainer for the Center for the Study of Learning and Teaching Styles, New York. He has had many articles published in national journals such as the *NASSP Bulletin, The Clearing House,* and *Educational Leadership.*

EILEEN D'ANNA is a high school English teacher in the Nanuet Union Free School District, New York, and a St. John's University Instructional Leadership doctoral candidate.

KENNETH DUNN is Professor and Chairperson, Department of Educational and Community Programs, Queens College, City University of New York. He is a former superintendent of schools and author or coauthor of 12 textbooks and more than 100 articles, monographs, chapters, management strategies, and instruments focused on administrative styles, learning styles, staff development, supervision, and teaching styles. The Dunns received the Education Press of America Award for the best series published in an educational journal (1977) and were the first husband and wife team to be elected simultaneously to the Hunter College Hall of Fame (1988).

RITA DUNN is Professor, Division of Administrative and Instructional Leadership, and Director of the Center for the Study of Learning and Teaching Styles, St. John's University, New York. She is author or coauthor of 18 textbooks and almost 300 published articles. Dr. Dunn is the recipient of many professional awards, including New York University's Research Scholarship Award, National Academy of Education Research Management Scholarship, the Mensa Education and Research Foundation Award for Excellence in Research, and St. John's University's Outstanding Faculty Achievement Gold Medal and highly competitive (first) Award for Excellence in Graduate Teaching (1995).

JENNIFER GALLAGHER is a teacher and Director of Youth Services at St. Brigid's School and Parish in Westbury, New York, and a St. John's University Instructional Leadership doctoral candidate.

JACK GREMLI is Director of Music (K–12) in the Nanuet Union Free School District, New York. He and the district were the 1996 recipients of the New York State Music Association's Presidential Citation for excellence in music education. He is a published author and a St. John's University Instructional Leadership doctoral candidate.

FRAN GUASTELLO is Principal, St. Brigid's School, Brooklyn, New York, and coauthor of *Our Wonderful Learning Styles,* the new global, multisensory learning-style assessment (K–5). She is a St. John's University Instructional Leadership doctoral candidate.

ROSE FRANCES LEFKOWITZ, MPA, RRA, is Associate Professor, State University of New York's Health Science Center at Brooklyn College of Health-Related Professions. She is a St. John's University Instructional Leadership doctoral candidate and has had several articles and a book published.

DIANE MITCHELL is a Clarkstown Central School District secondary teacher and a St. John's University Instructional Leadership doctoral candidate.

DEBORAH O'CONNELL-BREBBIA is a Clarkstown Central School District secondary science teacher and a St. John's University Instructional Leadership doctoral candidate.

PATRICIA M. RAUPERS is Coordinator of Staff Development Programs for the Northern Valley Schools, Demarest, New Jersey. She has had articles and instructional materials published and is a St. John's University Instructional Leadership doctoral candidate.

PATRICE H. ROBERTS, Staff Development Trainer, Northern Valley Schools, Demarest, New Jersey, is a St. John's University Instructional Leadership doctoral candidate and a certified staff trainer for the Center for the Study of Learning and Teaching Styles. She is also a published author.

MARJORIE S. SCHIERING is a teacher in the Stony Point Elementary School, North Rockland, New York, and the author of the Programmed Learning Sequence and Contract Activity Package on ecosystems published by St. John's University's Center for the Study of Learning and Teaching Styles, where she is a doctoral candidate in Instructional Leadership.

ANITA SOBOL is Assistant Principal, William H. Carr Junior High School #194, Queens, and a St. John's University Instructional Leadership doctoral candidate.

ILISA D. SULNER is a 20-year veteran educator and Principal of a New York City public school serving students (ages 5–15) with severe disabilities. She is a St. John's University Instructional Leadership doctoral candidate.

RITA GLASER TAYLOR is a Ramapo, New York, itinerant teacher and a St. John's University Instructional Leadership doctoral candidate. Her article describing the learning styles of deaf children was published in 1995.

ISBN 0-275-96066-8

90000>

9 780275 960667

EAN

HARDCOVER BAR CODE